Heart
and Home

Other books by Debra Evans

The Mystery of Womanhood
The Complete Book on Childbirth

Heart
and Home

A Reaffirmation
of Traditional Mothering

Debra Evans

CROSSWAY BOOKS • WESTCHESTER, ILLINOIS
A DIVISION OF GOOD NEWS PUBLISHERS

Mary Cassatt, *Mother Feeding Her Child,* pastel. The Metropolitan Museum of Art, From the collection of James Stillman, Gift of Ernest Dr. G. Stillman, 1922. (22.16.22)

First printing, 1988

Printed in the United States of America

Library of Congress Catalog Card Number 87-71894

ISBN 0-89107-464-3

To Joanna, Katherine, David, and Jonathan—
in celebration of fifteen years of motherhood.
> I love you, Jo.
> I love you, Katy.
> I love you, David.
> I love you, Jon.
>> Faithfully yours,
>> Mom

*Even the sparrow finds a home,
and the swallow has her nest,
where she rears her brood
beside thy altars,
O Lord of Hosts, my King and my God.
Happy are those who dwell in thy house;
they never cease from praising thee.*

Psalm 84: 3, 4, NEB

Contents

Acknowledgments

*T*HIS BOOK WAS WRITTEN IN RESPONSE to a request from my publisher, Lane Dennis, whose burden for the plight of today's young mothers prompted him to ask me to write a few words of encouragement in book form. The assignment gave me an opportunity to tap into a reservoir of thoughts, feelings, and experiences that I had wanted to put into words for a long time.

In addition, I must express deep gratitude to the many women I have had the privilege to share with as a childbirth educator, breastfeeding consultant, and friend. My life has been enriched tremendously through what I have learned from expectant, new, and experienced mothers. It has been quite an education for *all* of us!

Most importantly, a *big* thanks is hereby officially extended to my husband, Dave, and our four children. What else can I possibly say? You're all fantastic—and I love you very, very much.

Preface

*T*HIS BOOK WOULD NEVER HAVE BEEN WRITTEN if I had not received the gift of life through the woman who willingly gave birth to her first child (me) in 1953. Of this event, Nancy Allen Munger wrote:

> The first time I saw Debbie was when the nurse appeared around the curtain at 9:30 the morning of Wednesday, January 28th. My first impression was noise—she had her fist in her mouth sucking as loud as possible for an 8½-hour-old little girl. No one had shown me how to nurse her. I took the little bundle in my arms and placed her by my right side and presented her with her first dinner. The minute the nipple touched her lips she grabbed it and started sucking as if this were very customary! I could feel the milk, or rather secretion, come from my toes practically.
>
> During the next week in the hospital they brought her to me at 5:30 A.M., 9:30, 1:30, 5:30, and 9:30, omitting the midnight feeding. If anyone had told me I would enjoy being awake at 5:30 A.M. . . . ha! But this was different.
>
> My bed was next to the window and overlooked a beautiful white statue of Mary in the grotto at the front of St. Joseph's

Hospital. At night this was illuminated. I wonder if I'll ever again experience the deep contentment of those early-morning hours: my newborn at my breast looking up at me while I looked out at Mary and prayed thanks to God.

Just as my mother's glimpse into my own beginnings enables me to better understand her role in my life, this journal collection of reflections on mothering is designed to encourage others to more deeply appreciate the significance and meaning of motherhood in their lives. It is a gathering of thoughts and feelings gleaned from the past fifteen years, all written from the heart. Each part of this book explores a different dimension of what it's like to be a mother at this time and place in history. I invite you to share these chapters of my life: take from them what you will. May God's grace, strength, and peace be multiplied to you daily as you endeavor to live out His calling and bear witness to the power of His love to those around you.

Debra Evans

Introduction

*F*OUR THOUSAND YEARS AGO, a small group of
Jewish midwives rejected a royal decree
issued by an Egyptian Pharaoh. Designed to
diminish the fruitfulness of the Hebrew nation,
the command required the midwives to kill all
male children born with their assistance. Led by
two women named Shiphrah and Puah, their
resistance to the Pharaoh's order resulted in the
survival of a baby named Moses and, ultimately, to
the liberation of six hundred thousand Hebrew
slaves from four hundred years of captivity. For
their brave defiance, God made the midwives
prosperous in their work, bringing about an
increase in the Jewish population and blessing the
midwives with homes and families of their own.

As the first chapter of Exodus continues, we
see a powerful picture emerging as all of
Pharaoh's efforts to suppress Israel were thwarted
by the combined actions of women who were
willing to reach out while risking their lives to
save young children. Many Israelite women,
including Moses' mother and sister, became
involved in this conspiracy. Even Pharaoh's own
daughter provided sanctuary after Moses was
discovered along the riverbank, where he was
hidden in the rushes. The rescue and protection
of this one child, who would eventually lead his
people to freedom and become a key figure in

history, is a dramatic example of the power of mothering.

This story from the first two chapters of Exodus also provides a moving testimony to the role of motherhood. As I reflected on it, I found myself asking, What *is* motherhood? A calling? A career? A biological capability? An instinctive search for status? Or *a way of life,* a state of the mind and heart that compels women to open their arms, embrace, nourish, and protect?

Considering the vital role mothers have played in world culture, why doesn't it seem enough to be "just a mother" anymore? Have we forgotten what being a mother is all about and why mothering matters? In competing with men, have women also rejected the central position motherhood has held in all previous societies? Where have all the mothers gone, and why did they leave? Is having money more important than having children? Are things more valuable than people? Was what men were doing really that superior to what women were doing before all these changes took place?

I have often asked myself these questions and have struggled at times with my conclusions. Through it all, something within me has kept me close to my children, preventing me from feeling I could relinquish the role I have felt destined to play in their lives, especially during their formative years. Consequently, I've ended up a misfit, a rebel, and a kind of pioneer. So beware: the book you are about to read will jar as well as amuse you. The stories in it have been brought back from a strange wilderness made up of wrecks remaining from an ancient, worldwide tradition. As I've stumbled among these ruins, I have chosen to set up camp on the outskirts of an emerging brave new world. This new order appears to be undermining an entire way of being that women have shared throughout the centuries—the way of motherhood. We must not forget that in various cultures from the earliest times, it has been "just mothers" who have had the responsibility of welcoming and promoting new life.

Only mothers know what it means to have conceived, carried, birthed, nursed, and nurtured the most vulnerable among us. The bonds created by such activities, when allowed to take place with society's blessing, form the very foundations of human love.

Perhaps the title of this book should have been: *She Started Out a Mother and Ended up a Total Fanatic.* But would any but the most "radical" among us have wanted to read it? Whether I'll be considered a traitor by my generation or a saint by the next remains to be seen, but for now I wouldn't mind being known as a "tribal guardian," in the words of the late Selma Fraiberg. In her last book, *Every Child's Birthright,* Dr. Fraiberg called for an informed citizenry to protect and advance the rights of every child by considering each one worthy of mothering.[1] Like the women of Moses' time, what is needed is a determined resistance to stand up for the helpless among us, who do not have voices to tell us what mothering—what life itself—means to them. More importantly, if mothers choose to return to a way of life that allows them to more fully bond with and nurture their children, we must be more willing as a society and as the Body of Christ to support and encourage them in their endeavors.

The time has come to celebrate motherhood and to re-create an ethic that recognizes the worth and dignity of mothering within our society. We can't afford *not* to any longer.

A social anthropologist and mother of five wrote: "We have organized a society in which responsibility for healing, education, and birthing has been handed over to the professions. As a result the motherhood role has become impoverished. All too often the only personal satisfaction and social recognition that a woman can find is in a job outside the home. We have lost something precious. For being a mother is one of the most important jobs anyone can do. The future lies in the hands of mothers today."[2]

A song from the early seventies said it well: "Don't it always seem to go that you don't know what you've got 'til it's gone? They paved paradise and put up a parking lot!"[3] This book is my attempt to pry up some of the concrete that has been laid down in recent years before the beauty lying beneath it becomes even more difficult to find, obscured by our culture's endless quest for success. As mothers, *what we say and do matters for eternity,* not only within our families, but within the greater context of our society and, as we have seen, world history as well.

There is nothing more important to a nation than having its youngest citizens feel loved and accepted. My prayer is that more women will have the courage to follow their hearts and inspire others to join them in the process.

Love alone has entry to the secrets of God.

ONE

To an Expectant Mother

*E ven if you are a woman who has been
taught since childhood of a loving heavenly
Father, you may not be fully convinced that he
really loves* you, individually *and*
unconditionally. *During pregnancy, perhaps
more than at any other time of your life, you
need to be* fully convinced *of his love. You need
to rest in that love, allowing it to be the*
stabilizing factor for your life, *and for the life
of your family.* [1]

Mari Hanes

*T*ODAY YOU HEARD THE NEWS: A new life has begun!
Deep within your body, securely nestled in
your womb, your preborn child is developing
at such a rapid pace it's difficult to even
comprehend it. From the moment of conception,
your precious little one entered into a life that is
now unfolding under the loving hand of God.
Now the test has confirmed it—you really are
pregnant! Praise God for the child within you,

for the tiny son or daughter you are carrying, nurturing, protecting, and expecting! Truly this is an event worthy of a first-class celebration!

Although your due date may seem a long way off, the coming months will give you a chance to prepare your life for the arrival of your new baby. Before you know it, your baby's birth day will take place and you'll be holding this precious child in your arms. This time of waiting can be fruitful and rewarding as you move closer to that magnificent moment in time.

The Lord's design for fetal growth and development is very intricate, woven together in a beautiful way through many minute details. The physiological aspects of pregnancy—the various changes your body began to go through the instant your baby was conceived—are amazing! The many processes that will enable you to protect and nourish your child can give you confidence in God's design for your life. Emotional ups and downs and the discomforts of pregnancy, however, are less predictable and can be challenging to cope with at times.

During this pregnancy, you and your husband will have the opportunity to trust God in new ways as you rely on Him for guidance, protection, strength, and spiritual direction. Don't be surprised if you find yourselves confronted with inner conflict as you face doubts about your ability to be good parents, fears about childbirth, worries concerning the baby's development, or changes in your marital relationship. There may even be moments when you'll wonder if having this baby is worth it all! Bearing a child, whether your first or your tenth, will require both of you to lay aside your own comfort in many ways for the sake of expanding God's creation.

You will often reflect on the life forming

within you, wondering who this child will become, what he or she will look like, and how you will feel about taking on the responsibility of caring for your baby. These times will lead you into a deep awareness of your baby's developing life, thereby enhancing the process through which you will bond with your child. One of the highlights of your pregnancy will be when you hear the baby's heartbeat for the first time, so fast and yet so strong as it brings you further confirmation of the life you are carrying. Another landmark will be when you feel your baby move, a gentle flutter within your abdomen that will make you want to place your hand over his or her tiny body and say a prayer of thanksgiving for the privilege of encountering such indescribable joy.

The hormones circulating through your body will make you feel softer all over as your skin changes and your breasts begin to fill out in preparation for nurturing your baby through nursing. These changes will make you feel quite different from your usual self—more feminine, less independent, and very *maternal.* Just as you physically experience these changes, you will find your *heart* softening as well. You may find yourself crying more easily and opening up to the wonder of life all around you. Already, even before your baby arrives, he or she is teaching you about what it means to be a mother!

As you prepare for your baby's entry into your life, there may be times when you will feel weak, fatigued, frightened, tempted, or confused. That's normal! It isn't unusual to feel pulled in many directions by friends, family, and society. God doesn't expect you to ignore or deny these feelings. A quick trip through the Psalms will remind you that David, who was much loved by the Lord, felt free to share even his most desperate emotional struggles with God. There are numerous Psalms to encourage and uplift you in times of distress. Run to them whenever you feel burdened. Being a Christian doesn't confer some sort of "Super-Humanity" upon believers that exempts us from feeling a wide variety of emotions: it means, rather, that our foundation is to be based upon the solid rock of Jesus Christ. *Nothing* can separate you from His love! Through frequent prayer, study of God's Word, and quiet reflection on the majesty of your Creator, you will find in this pregnancy a time of renewed fellowship with the Lord. Learning to go to God with your arms wide open will help you to embrace His love for you anew each day.

Being human makes it easy to hug our concerns close to ourselves rather than trust God to care for us. It takes real effort to depend on our Heavenly Father to meet our needs. We must *choose* to walk with Him day by day as we get to know the Lord better, and talk with Him *often*. This pregnancy, your upcoming birth experience, and mothering this child will provide you with unlimited opportunities for spiritual growth, enabling you to become increasingly aware that God's Word is *true*. Realize that the Lord's grace will always be sufficient for you if you draw near to Him with a sincere heart, even when things happen that are unexpected or unpleasant. In all things, the comfort of the Holy Spirit will be present to sustain you.

These next several months will give you time to prepare and plan for your baby's birth in much the same way as your engagement period gave you a chance to get ready for your wedding. There are things you will need to consider as you plan to make this birth as safe and as special as possible: Where will the event take place? Who will attend the birth as your health care provider and support team? What things are important to you and your husband in terms of promoting your values and beliefs during the birth? There are numerous books, classes, maternal-child health advocates, and childbirth organizations to provide information for you to consider so that you can have a healthier and happier birth day. Take advantage of these resources! Protect your pregnancy by eating well, getting plenty of rest, and avoiding exposure to harmful substances such as cigarette smoke and alcohol in *any* amounts. Also, encourage your husband to assume a greater degree of responsibility for the health care decisions you will need to make by including him in your prenatal care and education to the fullest extent possible. It's easy for a man to feel like an outsider throughout this process, when in reality he is as much a part of it as you are! As the head of your household, his active participation in *all* aspects of your life is essential.

Most of all, enjoy these months of intimate sharing with your baby. Living in a culture that places little worth on the art of motherhood need not detract from your ability to savor the closeness you feel with your unborn child. Dream! Go for long walks! Sing to your baby! Pregnancy is not just a time of waiting and hoping. It's a time for *participating* in the exuberant joy of life. These will be remarkable, memorable months worth enjoying and experiencing to the fullest.

Congratulations . . . and welcome to mothering!

As the child within and your spirit are nourished, God's laws are set in motion. Growth is *natural* and *inevitable*. These months before delivery can add a quality to your life that will always remain with you. At the end of the gestation period, it is possible to be not only bulging with physical life, but brimming with spiritual life as well![2]

TWO

The Birthing Bed

The story is from everlasting to everlasting. Yet when it happens to you, that your new-born child is laid for the first time in your arms, it is the whole miracle of creation and your heart cries aloud as did Mary's: "My soul doth magnify the Lord." You know without being told that you are as near to touching the divine mystery as one may come in this life.[1]

Nell Dorr

DOWN IN OUR BASEMENT, behind a stack of boxes containing Christmas decorations, fabric scraps, and unmatched socks, a cherrywood bed frame leans against a cinder-block wall. Dust has coated it, having thickly gathered on the edges, but the hearts and flowers carved into the headboard can still be easily found winding their way across its top border. The mattress has been tossed out and two legs are splintered, making it incapable of supporting side boards. Yet, in spite of its condition, we continue to keep the bed

23

tucked away in its appointed place; we will probably never part with it. Out first child, a girl, was born in this bed, and when I look at the cherrywood with its flowery border, I remember her coming into the world.

I think about the day my mother called me and said, "I want to buy the bed my first grandchild will be born in." Soon after, she drove the half-hour distance to the farm I was living on and took me to an antique store to browse among its treasures. It was unusual at that time for my mother to buy me anything that costly, and I felt a familiar sense of dependency creeping up on me while shopping at her expense. Just the same, I didn't get a piece of furniture very often, and the thought of her offer to provide a new bed for us was delightful.

Up and down the aisles we stalked, peeking behind tall pine cupboards, massive walnut buffets, and ornately carved oak cabinets. We didn't see many beds on our search. The ones we did look at were either outrageously expensive brass affairs or were too small for a double-sized mattress. On the far wall of the store stood a bed we eventually agreed would be the perfect choice. It was only fifty dollars, so my mom generously proposed that I pick out a dresser to go with it.

When the two pieces arrived, they were a welcome addition to our home, which was decorated with hand-me-downs from both our families, Salvation Army artifacts, and garage sale discoveries. Once the bed's varnish was stripped off, the beauty of the cherrywood fully revealed itself, absorbing the wax I rubbed into it with ease. Our baby was due on June 28th, 1972. The birthing bed was finished and set up somewhere around the first of that month.

Often I would sit at the edge of the bed and gaze at the cradle nearby, trying to imagine what it would be like to have a baby living in the room with us. I pictured myself feeding and bathing her, taking her for walks, telling her stories. The dreams of an expectant mother about her preborn child, filled with awe and wonder, doubt and apprehension, are softened by a hopeful anticipation of days to come. As springtime gave way to summer, I felt myself blooming inside, and an urge to settle in and "nest" was always close at hand.

The pregnancy had begun tenuously. The previous fall, while visiting an out-of-town friend, I went into a free clinic for a checkup and diagnosis. I strongly suspected I was pregnant when my breasts began to feel tender and I felt queasy a great deal of the time. The doctors who examined me were confused by the size of my uterus, which they said was not as large as it should be for the dates I had given them. They suggested I go to the university hospital nearby, where I was promptly examined by three more doctors. I was told it might be a tubal pregnancy and that I should see my regular physician back home as soon as possible. All of the poking and prodding irritated and concerned me; the doctors' clinical attitude denied my inner awareness of what was happening within my body and directly contradicted the way I felt pregnancy should be approached.

The next day I began bleeding. In response to five exams? Perhaps. Certain that I was going to miscarry, I rushed to see my gynecologist, who kept telling me jokes and funny stories while he examined me. Is this the way some people deal with the possibility of death? Couldn't he see that I was afraid of losing my baby?

The doctor told me that I might in fact miscarry, but that a shot of a hormone which could possibly prevent this from happening would be helpful. After the injection, the nurse told me to go home and rest for a few weeks and to call if I had any concerns or questions. Her tone was much gentler and had a calming affect on my frazzled nerves.

My pregnancy continued with occasional spotting. The longer I went, the more attached to my baby I felt. Because of repeated confinements to bed in the early months, I read as many books on pregnancy and birth as I could find. During the winter I read *Childbirth Without Fear* by Grantly Dick-Read and *Painless Childbirth* by Fernand Lamaze. Since my mother had used the Lamaze method for the birth of my youngest sister in 1963, I had been brought up to believe that having a baby was a natural, normal aspect of female sexuality that I need not fear. My mom told me that she didn't take as much as an aspirin during her labor with Nancy and that all I would need to do is learn to relax and breathe properly to get through labor with a minimum amount of discomfort. A Lamaze instructor later cautioned us never to use the word *pain* to refer to labor, because the expectation of pain inevitably led to failure with the method. Both Lamaze's book and the instructor who shared with us stated that if performed correctly, the method would prevent pain entirely. At that point, I had no reason to doubt their claims and chose to believe that what they said was true.

With this kind of background, I fearlessly approached my upcoming labor, expecting it to be the peak experience of my life. I thought I had solved the problem of labor pain, and since the pregnancy proceeded along well after the initial

scare with bleeding, I began to look for a
physician who would attend the birth of our baby
in our home. Why not? To me Ashley Montagu's
lectures and book *Touching* said it all: the most
unsanitary place in the city to give birth, next to a
garbage dump, is in a hospital, which is filled
with foreign bacteria, dreadful diseases, and toxic
chemicals. Why would any healthy woman want
to bring new life into the world in a place such as
that?

In February I went to a breastfeeding support
group's monthly meeting and promptly inquired if
any of the women there were aware of a doctor
who attended home births. It just so happened
that several of the women had been to a Seventh-
Day Adventist doctor who gave his clients *a
choice* as to their baby's place of birth between
home and hospital. I set up an appointment with
him the next day. It was true—the very first thing
he asked me was how the pregnancy was going
and where I wanted to give birth. I couldn't
believe it! It turned out that he had been a
missionary in Africa for much of his life, and he
found American homes to be wonderful places to
deliver babies in as long as the mother had had a
healthy pregnancy. His fee? For all of the prenatal
care, the home birth, and my six-week checkup,
the total bill was $250.

As our child's birth day approached, I
continued to read, attend the breastfeeding
support group I had joined, and talk to other
women who had young children. I entered an
entirely new world, one I had been completely
unaware of before. It seemed like a culture within
a culture, made up of creative, resourceful
women, lovely babies, an endless amount of
mother/infant folklore, and a brand of wisdom I
had only remotely been acquainted with

previously. The more I learned, the more I wanted
to keep exploring, listening, absorbing. Something
drew me to those women. I felt comfortable
around them as my abdomen swelled and as I felt
myself drawing apart from a society that viewed
my experience as nothing to be excited about,
certainly nothing special. My preparation for
motherhood had begun in earnest.

The last four weeks of my pregnancy, however,
were fairly miserable. The baby within me
prevented me from sleeping soundly, exerted
constant pressure on my bladder and rectum, and
squirmed restlessly as if to let me know that she
was reaching the limit of my capacity to provide
enough space and nourishment for her. I
frequently wept with frustration and yearned to
hold my baby in my arms. It seemed like she was
never going to arrive at all, that I would just
continue to grow larger, that there would be no
end to the heaviness in my abdomen. Then on the
afternoon of our baby's due date, labor finally
began.

After a bout with diarrhea, I noted a tight
feeling in my pubic area that strongly resembled
menstrual cramps, except that it forcefully
radiated toward my back and felt like heat waves
that would slowly build in intensity, then taper
off. When I went to use the toilet again, I noticed
blood on the tissue and panicked. Was it normal
to feel this intestinal discomfort and be bleeding
at the same time? I called the doctor, who briefly
evaluated what I told him over the phone and
reassured me that everything sounded normal. He
asked me to go to his office so he could check my
progress. Remembering to relax and breathe
slowly and deeply with contractions, I phoned my
husband at the first opportunity and suggested he
meet me at the doctor's office. He later told me

that during the phone call, he put his cup of coffee down on a table that turned out not to be there and then went flying in our Volkswagen bug to Dr. Marsa's.

I had some initial difficulty finding a ride, but finally located a friend of ours who picked me up in a 1964 Falcon with four bald tires. We proceeded to travel over several miles of gravel roads, which probably had a stimulating effect on my labor overall. All the while, I kept breathing and relaxing with a perfectly deadpan "Lamaze look" on my face during contractions.

The doctor didn't seem surprised when I told him I was feeling pretty uncomfortable in spite of the Lamaze techniques. He checked my cervix, which was two-thirds dilated, and explained that the slight bit of bleeding I was having was a normal response of the cervix to being stretched open. I was excited, apprehensive, and exhilarated all at the same time. On the way home, we noticed the tank was below empty and stopped to put a little gas in the car. I wanted to shout out to the attendant, "My baby's going to be born in just a couple of hours!" Although I'd never met the man, I thought he ought to know.

When we got home, I stripped off my clothes and got into the shower, letting the warm water spray on my back. As a contraction would start, I would lean against the wall and take slow, deep, full breaths to attempt to relieve the pressure in my abdomen. It still hurt. The pain puzzled me at first, then annoyed me. I thought of the prayer that asks God for help because "the sea is so wide and my boat is so small." To me, my baby seemed awfully wide and my pelvis and birth canal small in comparison! At any rate, the analogy seemed to fit.

Up until this point, my husband's presence as

a passive bystander had suited me just fine. Suddenly I wanted him with me right away and didn't want him to leave *ever again*. He rubbed my back, helped me breathe, played his guitar, and smiled a lot. "Why am *I* the one who has to go through this?" I thought as I threw up my orange juice. "I will never have another baby again. And maybe not even sex." The otherness of Dave's masculine nature seemed distant and unrelated to what I was experiencing, but somehow I longed for him to reach beyond the void between us and feel what I was feeling. I knew that having him right there next to me was as close as a man could possibly come to understanding the work of birth.

For a brief span of three hours, space and time changed. I often felt helpless to manage my pain and bewildered by a body that was supposed to be cooperating with my mind more efficiently during labor. I wanted to give up, set my body on a shelf, and walk away.

But cope I did. A strange inner strength I had never been aware of emerged as I rode the wild waves of my contractions, willing my body to open up and let my child pass through. When I began to push, my entire being was swept along by the tidal rhythms of my uterus, moving my baby down, pressing the muscles of my pelvis open, filling every possible space with an unrelenting force that seemed to care nothing for the wishes of my mind. When a contraction would begin, I would brace myself on my knees as I knelt on our bed. With a groan, I would follow the dictates of my womb as it tightened itself from the top down. Then a blissful two to three minutes of rest would flood my body as one contraction would end and enable me to prepare myself for the next.

Outside, through the open windows in our room, I listened to the sounds of dogs barking and birds singing. The air was filled with the stillness of twilight as the sun began to set. I breathed in its fragrance and let the coolness caress my forehead. How strange it seemed that this was just an ordinary day, filled with ordinary events, when at that moment I was involved in the most demanding effort of my life.

"Not much longer," said the doctor quietly as he prepared to receive the baby. Then I heard my husband tell me, "I can see the baby's hair! Keep pushing! You can do it! Oh wow . . ." I doubted them both, thinking, "This isn't my baby—it's an immovable object that has no right to be where it is, and all I want to do is get it out! Now!"

But then an amazing thing happened, a most unusual and wonderful thing. The pain gave way to relief as my daughter's head appeared. Such *blessed* relief! Then her shoulders came through and the incredible reality of what was taking place hit me full force, all at once, as I felt her arms, her back, and her legs slip through in a whoosh, all moist with amniotic fluid, her warm skin so soothing in its lovely smoothness.

"It really *is* a baby after all . . . my baby, my baby, my baby," I thought as I reached out to touch her as the doctor laid her next to me. "I am really a mother at last."

For the next forty-eight hours, sleep would not come. I felt myself coming fully alive to my daughter, and I didn't want to miss a moment of what was happening . . .

The first thing I noticed was the creamy substance that coated her from head to toe like a silky garment protecting her skin from the harshness of the cool air enveloping her body. Her cries called forth a new tone in my voice, a high-pitched sort of cooing, as I sought to comfort the little one whom I had never met before.

But I had *known* her. Welcoming her home was simply an extension of maternal hospitality, an expansion of the knowledge I already possessed about the person whose body had begun within my own nine months before. I knew her movements, how they felt, how she physically expressed herself long before I saw her for the first time. Our heartbeats had communicated in synchrony from the first beat of her tiny heart four weeks into the pregnancy. Without any planning on my part, I had sent a continual supply of nutrients to her in just the right amounts during her gestation. From conception, she had been her own unique self and, until now, had completely relied upon me for shelter and sustenance. A part of me grieved as I realized we would never be so close again, and from that point on she would be moving *away* from me. A mother gives birth not once, but twice. Now that the initial letting go was over, God would have to help me with the rest.

Oblivious to others in the room, I marveled at the warmth of Joanna's small body as she snuggled next to me. Then she looked into my eyes and listened to my voice. "Yes, yes, here I am, my sweet baby. There's no need to cry. Shhh . . . there, there now. Everything is all right. Here I am."

Her umbilical cord was tied and cut and the placenta birthed—an afterthought, it seemed to me. Dave called my parents and his mother. They brought a bottle of pink champagne and acted silly. There were six of us born that evening: one baby, two parents, and three grandparents. None of us were quite sure how to act under the circumstances, but we were all very pleased and happy to be there together, a family in transition. Several friends stopped in to say hello. It truly was a one-of-a-kind birth day celebration!

One by one, everyone went home. The doctor told me to call him if anything unusual came up. My mother said she would bring out a ham and some cheesecake for me to munch on as I recovered. Through all the commotion, Joanna nursed contentedly, as if to say her birth had been a perfectly logical next step in her existence. Amidst flowers and gifts and bows and wrapping paper I wondered how long it would take to resume a normal pattern of life again.

Dave poured me a glass of water and set some juice by the bed, then asked if I minded if he slept on the couch. He looked exhausted, and I didn't have the heart to tell him I was wide awake or that Joanna showed no signs of slowing down her activity at my breast. With the bedroom all to myself, I entered the night full of wonder, ready to learn. I knew more about world history, geometry, and the Beatles than I did about mothering, but that didn't stop me. We had no schedules to meet, no routines to adopt, no interruptions. As I look back on my introduction to mothering, it occurs to me that it was one of the holiest moments of my life. Feeling peaceful and full of thanksgiving, I greeted the dawn with my daughter lying closely beside me. I will never forget the sense of absolute tranquillity I discovered in that sunrise.

How could it be that the happiest moments of my life had sprung from my greatest pain? That I felt like laughing and crying at the same time so often during those first few days of my daughter's life? So many emotions stirred within my heart! The sense of awe I felt, that two small cells had become our child, overwhelmed me. Simultaneously, I felt a heavy weight of responsibility for her brand-new life falling right between my shoulders. I alternately smiled and wept. I shed tears of concern while grinning with joy. Birth, I found, is a bittersweet moment, when heaven and earth collide in a profusion of possibilities, hopes, and expectations. I knew that I would never be quite the same again.

Looking back, I am convinced that God made babies to be lovable, even durable, as a way of helping their parents. Babies thrive on their mother's milk and the tender, loving care expressed through cuddling, rocking, singing, bathing, stroking, and being kept close by. A baby's needs and wants seem to be inseparable until later in the first year of life. As I responded to her needs for nourishment, protection, warmth, and physical affection on a daily basis, Joanna taught me much of what I needed to know about mothering. I was fortunate to be in an environment which fostered this ability, allowing me to discover how to nurture my daughter in a flexible, spontaneous way.

The days somehow have managed to merge into a string of fifteen years, and now Joanna is getting ready to start high school. She is sixty-five inches tall (where is the little girl I was once able to cradle in my arms?), weighs a hundred and twelve pounds (what happened to the baby I carried in her backpack for hours on end?), and wears a size 8 shoe (what would she say if I kissed her toes now?). She is an independent, strong-willed, and sensitive young woman. I continue to be challenged by her, watch over her, pray for her, and be amazed by her. As I feel the proverbial apron strings loosening, part of me

wants to call back the years that have come
between us and to return to those moments when
she would look up at me with her gentle eyes in
recognition of our closeness. I can only return in
my dreams and thank God that I was able to live
my life in such a way that my daughter could
depend on me so completely as an infant.

So now the bed sits downstairs, strung with
cobwebs until I remember to brush them off
every once in a while. Dave's mom has fourteen
grandchildren, and we account for nearly a third
of them. Our children, who could only be
imagined and hoped for when I picked the bed
out of the rows of furniture in the antique store,
are now living and breathing among us, and it is
impossible to remember fully what our lives were
like without them.

A philosopher named Tagore once said, "I have
had my invitation to this world's festival, and thus
my life has been blessed. My eyes have seen and
my ears have heard. . . . It was my part at this
feast to play upon my instrument, and I have done
all I could."

Becoming a mother opened up my eyes and
ears more fully to the grand symphony of life. I
am still looking, still listening, and still learning.

> There were two and now there's a third
> human being, a new spirit, finished and
> complete, unlike the handiwork of man; a
> new thought and a new love. . . . It's
> positively frightening. . . . And there's
> nothing grander in the world.
>
> Feodor Dostoevsky

THREE

Snuggles

They told me babies should not be held;
  It would spoil them and make them cry.
I wished to do what is best for them,
  And the years sped quickly by.

Now empty are my yearning arms;
  No more the thrill sublime.
If I had my babies back again,
  I'd hold them all the time.

Written by an American
mother in the 1920s

*I*N 1894, AN EMINENT PEDIATRICIAN FROM NEW YORK, Dr. Luther Emmett Holt, published a book that shook the art of mothering down to its very foundations. Titled *The Care and Feeding of Children,* Holt's book influenced several generations of moms to avoid the "unnecessary and vicious . . . and sometimes injurious" habit of rocking their infants to sleep. His solution? Replace the cradle with a stationary crib!

Dr. Holt also was responsible for starting the rumor that mothers should not pick their babies up when they cried. His rationale? It would "spoil" an infant if this were done. And what else did the dear doctor contribute to the history of infant care in the United States? He also persuaded mothers to feed their baby by the clock instead of by demand since too much handling of the baby was to be avoided.

This self-proclaimed "expert" on mothering, lacking any scientific evidence to support his recommendations, should have been run out of the country on the spot. Instead, his book sold thousands of copies to women who believed Dr. Holt presented a better way to care for infants, one that must have seemed thoroughly modern in comparison to practices that had been passed along for countless generations. With scarcely a protest, some of the most enjoyable and rewarding aspects of mothering were overthrown.

What type of man was he? In a biography published in *Pediatric Profiles* in 1957, written by Dr. Holt's last assistant and the assistant's collaborators, he was described as "a highly efficient and perfectly coordinated human machine . . . austere and unapproachable." Holt's secretary could not recall that the doctor had ever said "Good Morning," nor was he known to ever praise anyone or anything. Independence, self-reliance, and the avoidance of dependence on the affections of others later became the goal of behaviorists following in Holt's footsteps, who seemed to treat children as mechanical objects one could "condition" as one pleased. Consequently, in homes all over America, an unnatural and disturbing approach to mothering replaced the loving nurture which had been an integral part of family life for centuries.

Thankfully, current research has proved the fallacy of Holt's claims. Due to the pioneering work of Dr. Harry Harlow in the late fifties and early sixties, Dr. John Bowlby in the late sixties, and pediatricians Marshall Klaus and John Kennell in the seventies, the importance of touch between mothers and infants has been validated. What mothers have known since the beginning of time has finally been shown to be healthful for babies after all. These researchers, and many others as well, have found that babies cry less and gain weight better when held and rocked in the arms of their mothers. (Surprise, surprise!) Also, they say mothers end up feeling closer and more attached to their infants when they feed their babies on demand and snuggle up close to them. (You're kidding!)

Unfortunately, the myth of spoiling remains. Since at least two generations of mothers were saturated in the theories of the behaviorists, it is still somewhat suspect if a mother wishes to stay home and rock her baby, tote her infant with her wherever she goes, or snuggle up to her little one at night. We've even devised all sorts of odd contraptions to act as substitutes for mothers' arms: windup swings, plastic infant carriers, and strollers, to name a few. Whatever happened to cradles, cloth carriers, and rocking chairs? Here and there a few may be seen, but for the most part, in our culture babies still spend the majority of their time away from the bodies of their mothers.

Is there any reason to keep a baby moving? Yes! Rocking movement, it turns out, just happens to produce a number of beneficial effects on both babies *and* adults: cardiac output increases, aiding circulation; digestive function is enhanced, reducing constipation and gas buildup; respiration is promoted, discouraging lung congestion; and brain activity is triggered which reduces anxiety and brings about stress reduction. Moving to and fro with one's baby makes complete sense from a physiological point of view. When added to the emotional benefits produced by close physical contact with one's infant, we can safely say at last that Dr. Luther Emmett Holt was, at least on this point, totally off his rocker.

Why were millions of mothers convinced Holt was right? I think at least part of it had to do with the way the American public came to view the advice of "the experts" in the forties and fifties. Not only in pediatrics, but in obstetrics as well, mothers were coerced unwittingly into giving birth and nurturing their babies in the most unnatural and unreasonable ways. Drugged and left alone during labor and put out with gas anesthetics for birth, their babies were born with forceps and carried away to nurseries for supervision. In addition to the rapid decline in successful breastfeeding, these practices all became the hallmarks of "modern" maternity care. Subsequently, an entire generation of women was robbed of some of the most meaningful experiences of their lives.

Ashley Montagu once stated the crux of the problem perfectly when he said, "What is humanly wrong cannot be professionally right." It was humanly wrong to deny infants the right to be held, stroked, cuddled, and rocked by their mothers. It was humanly wrong to remove birth out from under the authority of the family and place it on the altar of modern medicine. It was humanly wrong for a man to assume he could even come close to figuring out how to improve on mothering behavior without spending at least twenty years "mothering" children on a daily, full-time basis himself. In removing the key elements of maternal satisfaction from maternal experience, women were left with an artificial, undignified sterile approach to their most

important vocation, and soon after began to depart
from their role by the thousands.

So when others tell you that you might spoil
your baby by holding her too much, ignore them
and go right ahead and snuggle. When your kids
are sick or tired or lonely or feeling lost and want
to curl up next to you, don't worry—just snuggle.
When you're tempted to abandon your baby to a
dark room to try to get him to sleep, what
admonition should ring inside your ear? You've
got it: "Snuggle!"

While raising my children, I often found
myself being challenged to justify my approach to
mothering to well-meaning relatives, friends, and
doctors. But what was I actually defending? *The
right to be close to my babies.* Looking back, I
can hardly believe the things people felt
compelled to say:

> "If you're not careful, your daughter is going
> to become too dependent on you!"

> "You really ought to leave him more often so
> he'll get used to being with others." (At eight
> weeks?)

> "You should never let your baby sleep with
> you. Don't you know she'll become sexually
> confused?"

I firmly believe that each mom needs to do what
is best with her children. I recognize that some
moms don't snuggle, or can't snuggle, or think
snuggling is weird. But for those of us who
downright enjoy snuggling and rocking and
cuddling and nuzzling our babies, please don't
use Holt's poppycock to try to prove us "wrong."

Acting as if a mother can damage her children with tender loving care is nonsense.

Touch, taste, hearing, pressure, eye contact, and warmth are all essential components of maternal-infant interaction that enable children to grow into their abilities to love and care for others. When deprived of these things, babies can fail to thrive and may actually die. As an infant's senses come into contact with his mom's body and he begins to experience her communication with him through her eyes, facial expressions, sounds she makes, and snuggles she gives him, *real* attachment takes place. It's a back and forth process: I look at you, you look back at me; I speak, you wiggle and smile; I touch you, you get to know me; I respond to your cries, you discover you can trust me to meet your needs. This is a spectacularly choreographed set of exchanges that teaches a mother how to comfort and satisfy her baby while teaching the baby what it means to be accepted and loved. Mothers are very, very good at this when not belittled or ridiculed for doing what often comes so naturally; and babies are born with the power to elicit such responses!

I am absolutely convinced that God designed mothering to be *rewarding* to mothers. To me, all of the hundreds of hours I have spent holding and nursing and snuggling my children make up much of what has been gentle, sweet, and lovely in my life. To this day I can't walk by a baby without longing to sweep her in my arms and hug her! And even though my kids are much older now, I still have to touch and hug them oodles of times each day. We give one another back rubs and facial massages and kisses and caresses all the time. Just because they're "big" doesn't mean they

have outgrown physical expressions of my love
for them, nor have I outgrown my *own* need for
affirmation through touch.

While my parents were living in Mexico for a
few years I had the chance to go down and visit
them for about ten days. I was so impressed! I've
never seen so much hugging! Families go
everywhere together, which often bothered my
very American folks. They would invite a friend to
dinner and end up hosting the entire clan. Even
older schoolchildren would walk arm in arm.
When I returned to the States, the first thing I
noticed was how *serious* and *cold* everyone
looked. They seemed so physically and
emotionally isolated from those around them. It's
a pity that Dr. Holt is no longer around to view
the fruits of his work.

One of my favorite mental pictures of Jesus is
thinking about the passage in the New Testament
where He gathers the little children into His arms
and blesses them. He would have made a great
daddy! It's obvious from the text that our Lord
enjoyed being in the company of children and
expected us to become more like them. What
better way than tickle "fights"? Playing peek-a-
boo? Running through the sprinkler together on a
hot day? Sitting in a rocking chair and reading a
favorite book with one another? And yes,
snuggling. Go ahead—indulge. You won't regret
it as long as you live. Children who are snuggled
eventually grow up, move away, and often
produce grandchildren who will enjoy being
snuggled. The possibilities are endless.

Infancy and toddlerhood cover such a brief
span of time. Providing a secure beginning to a
child's life by being there *responsively* is a
worthwhile investment and is one that *every* mom

can enjoy if she gives herself permission to snuggle.

Anyone can be paid to do the physical work of rearing children, but only Mother can daily add the other dimensions. This is what makes her role so special to the daily life experience of her children.[1]

FOUR

Affecting Eternity

*C*hristian couples who have the faith to have
larger families today are making a
revolutionary statement and are contributing
in a vital way to the expansion of God's
Kingdom within the world. . . . Realize that you
(as a wife, mother, homemaker) are making
a vital contribution, one that cannot be
measured with a dollar sign. . . . It's a task that
can engage every ounce of creativity you have,
and produce satisfactions that endure for all
eternity.[1]

John Jefferson Davis

*O*N THE NIGHT BEFORE KATHERINE'S ARRIVAL . . .
It's 10 at night, and I know I should be
sleeping, but I feel just like I used to on the night
before Christmas—excited, nervous, curious. . . .

Tomorrow morning we plan to go into the
hospital to have our second child, after nine
months of waiting for our baby's birth day to
arrive.

At the doctor's office this afternoon, my
obstetrician did an exam and discovered that my
cervix is more than five centimeters dilated.

Rather than waiting for labor to begin on its own, he suggested that I meet him while he's on duty at the hospital. Since he won't be "on call" again for a couple of weeks, Dave and I decided to allow him to induce labor. Because I'm technically halfway through labor as it is, we would prefer to have Dr. Meils there than any of the other physicians in his practice.* And besides, we're both *more* than ready to get this show on the road and meet our new son or daughter.

Cuddled against me is our twenty-seven-month-old daughter, Joanna, sound asleep after an active day spent going to an art fair, the doctor's, and out to dinner. As I watch her peacefully resting by my side, I can't imagine how I'm going to love the new baby as much as I love her tonight. This pregnancy has been so different from Jo's . . . I guess I've been a lot busier than I thought I would be. Tonight will be our last night for being "just the three of us." After tomorrow, things will never be the same for our daughter again.

Looking down at her soft blonde curls, I wonder why I've put her in this position. Although I should know better, in some ways it seems like I'm betraying her! Do other moms ever feel this way when they have their second child? A part of me longs to keep things the way they are and not ever share myself with another child. Haven't I found it challenging enough to just meet *Joanna's* needs?

How will I manage the timing of each of their naps every day? Or taking two children who are both in diapers grocery shopping? Will Dave and I

*Since Katherine's birth in September 1974 numerous studies have pointed to the risks associated with the elective induction of labor for personal convenience rather than medical necessity. We would not choose this option today.

ever recover our sense of closeness once we're faced with so many more demands on our time? I realize that it's a little late to be asking these questions, but I'm suddenly feeling overwhelmed by this baby's imminent arrival. I'm not ready to go through labor again. (But will I ever be?) I'm afraid I won't love this baby as much as I love Joanna. And what if he or she isn't healthy—will I be able to cope? Oooops . . . there's another kick, a timely reminder that I better get to sleep before I attempt to figure out things that can only be *lived* through in order to be worked through. Tomorrow's going to be a very busy day . . .

> When I felt that my foot was slipping,
> thy love, O Lord, held me up.
> Anxious thoughts may fill my heart,
> but thy presence is my joy and my
> consolation.[2]

On the night after Katherine's arrival . . .

How thankful I am for all that has happened today, for this baby snuggled up beside me, for the gift of this new life! Words can't express the joy I feel tonight as I hold my child in my arms, touch her silky hair, kiss her chubby cheeks, and cry these tears of relief—relief that all has gone so well and that I already feel so much a part of my new daughter.

Do I feel the same as when Joanna was born? No . . . because this time I'm welcoming my baby as an *experienced* mother, who is already very familiar with nursing and bathing and diaper changing. It's so much more *comfortable* to hold a newborn now. It feels natural, even normal. Her presence reassures and soothes me. With Jo, all of this was totally brand-new, but now I have

hundreds of days' worth of mothering to draw
upon as I extend my love to this little girl.

As soon as labor began, I knew I could do this
again. I feel so close to the Lord! His presence has
sustained and upheld me all day. I want to shout
His praises so everyone in this hospital knows
who it is that has given me the strength and the
ability to birth and nurture this precious baby! An
individual has arrived unlike any other, so
different from her sister, so special to her parents.
We have named her Katherine Laurel after
welcoming her into our family this afternoon,
following a very quick two-and-a-half-hour labor,
and then happily watching her respond to life as
she calmly looked around for a little while and
then promptly fell asleep.

> Gracious is the Lord and righteous,
> our God is full of compassion.
> The Lord preserves the simple-hearted;
> I was brought low and he saved me.
> Be at rest once more, my heart,
> for the Lord has showered gifts upon you.[3]

In the weeks that followed Katy's birth . . .

There have been many surprises since Katy and
I returned home after an overnight stay at
Crittenton Hospital. I've been more emotional
than I usually am, with tears flowing
unexpectedly at odd hours during the day and
night. I do feel a change has taken place between
Joanna and me, but I know that it was inevitable.
What I hadn't planned on was how much closer
Dave and Jo would become. He spends most of
his free time taking her on errands, outings, and
assorted adventures to give me a chance to rest

and have time alone with Katy. I appreciate his active participation tremendously!

During the past several weeks, we've had to deal with Dave's sister's wedding and moving to a new house in addition to adjusting as a family to a new baby. It would be so wonderful if babies could be born in perfectly peaceful surroundings without having to deal with *"real* life" at the same time as taking on the responsibility for a *new* life. The stresses and strains aren't easy to cope with, and some days I find myself stretched to the utmost of my ability to make it through each day intact.

But whenever I look at Joanna as she busily empties out her cupboard in the kitchen or Katy as she smiles up at me with delight, I am reminded of their central importance in my life and of the value of their being here with me. These days we're walking through together will matter for eternity, and I must daily remind myself of the incomparable worth of my daughters to the personal Creator who has blessed me with the opportunity to be their mother.

What satisfaction there is in knowing that what I am doing *counts*. Although it would be nice to feel more appreciated at times, I don't need anyone to tell me where my children came from or where they're going. *I am certain of the value of their lives.* Within my heart lies a type of knowledge that no number of books, university courses, or logical arguments could have produced. *It is the knowledge of the significance of life itself, and of what it means to reflect the image of God in human form.*

> The Lord will accomplish his purpose for
> me. Thy true love, O Lord, endures for ever;
> leave not thy work unfinished.[4]

In the years that have followed Katy's birth . . .

Having a second child *did* change our family forever. There were as many lessons to be learned through mothering Katy and Joanna *together* as there had been in mothering Joanna alone. It is a good thing that most mothers don't have all two or three or four of their first children all at the same time! That *would* be very difficult to handle. But just as the nine months of pregnancy prepare a mother's heart for nurturing her expected baby, the months and years that follow that baby's arrival prepare her for each successive child. Dr. Herbert Ratner has said that it's a shame so many parents stop having children after they have two. Why? Because they only begin to fully adjust to their roles and get good at what they are doing on the *third* time around!

This may sound a bit judgmental, but I fully concur with Dr. Ratner. I became ever so much more relaxed, competent, and at ease with my nurturing role within our family as I went *beyond* the two I felt were *expected* of me and delved into mothering our third and fourth children afterwards. For myself, I can't seriously listen to mothering advice if it's being given by someone who has never had children or has had less than three children. This is due to the fact that two children are entirely manageable in comparison to the effort required to mother three or five or ten children. Also, a mother of two has no idea of the complexity of caring for a large family! I am always reminded of this when two or three of our children are gone for dinner and only three or four of us are sitting around the table. It's quieter . . . there are fewer dishes to wash . . . less food to buy and prepare. . . . In other words, it's a lot less hassle!

Opening up one's heart to having a larger family involves risk-taking, sacrifice, physical discomfort, and an abiding respect for the meaning of human life. Is the hassle worth it? Is each child important to God? Will the lives that we welcome into our families be lives that exist for eternity? Only you can answer these questions as you prayerfully consider their significance in your own life. I believe the answer is *yes,* and the children I sometimes struggle to care for and lovingly nurture are my affirmative response to the assurance I feel that their lives have been worth the effort.

> To thee I offer my outspread hands,
> Athirst for thee in a thirsty land.
> Show me the way that I must take;
> To thee I offer all my heart.[5]

FIVE

Of Lullabies and Exultations

The true harvest of my daily life is somewhat as intangible and indescribable as the tints of morning or evening. It is a little stardust caught, a segment of the rainbow I have clutched.

Henry David Thoreau,
Walden

OUTSIDE OUR KITCHEN WINDOW, one of nature's tender dramas has been unfolding before us at mealtimes as we sit and watch the evergreen tree at the corner of our front porch: in the closing days of March, a robin has chosen a pine bough only a few feet from our home to build her nest in.

The first time we noticed her, the robin was carrying wisps of string and shreds of paper to a secluded nook near the tree's trunk. Piece by piece, our small neighbor transported an odd assortment of materials to their destination. Soon after, we witnessed the demise of her bare-bones dwelling as two blue jays swooped in to tear the robin's creation apart. These jays, the bullies of our local bird world, had the audacity to attack an innocent robin's nest! Our children looked on

53

while the jays darted in and out of the branches, poking and pecking in a flurry of wings and tail feathers, jabbing here and there at the frantic robin as she defended her precious territory. Though outnumbered and outflanked, the single female held her ground. After the jays departed, she continued to go about her business, seemingly unruffled by the temporary intrusion.

Later in the afternoon, our friend faced additional trauma. An unseasonably forceful thunderstorm blew into the Midwest, pouring buckets of rain all over eastern Nebraska in general and directly onto our evergreen in particular. Down went the nest, collapsing under sheets of rain released from an anonymous storm cloud as it passed by. The robin was nowhere to be seen for the next few days as the miserable weather continued. Even hail came popping out all over at one point; flash floods were reported. Once again reminded why people never speak of moving to Lincoln for its climate, we forgot about the robin and tried to be friendly to each other in spite of getting drenched every time we stepped out the door for three days in a row.

While eating breakfast this morning, I happened to glance up toward the pine and what do you think I saw sitting there? In its original place, familiar bits of grass and debris were perched in the center of the tree. Our winged mother-to-be was still at it. Apparently undaunted by the whims of the elements, the bird had begun rebuilding for the second time, peeping and chirping all the while. As I pulled out of the driveway to take the kids to school, Joanna noticed the robin hard at work again and asked, "Hasn't she learned *yet?*" (My children have still to learn such tenacity when it comes to manual labor.)

After returning home, I watched the robin for a while. By all outward appearances, she actually seemed happy, literally whistling as she worked, bouncing all over the place searching for construction materials. Was it just my imagination or was she dancing? After the rain, worms abound in our area. Perhaps this was all her festival of thanksgiving.

I'm truly amazed by this robin's dedication. I marvel that she bothered to come back at all, let alone to the *exact same place* in our tree, or should I say *her* tree. Why? Don't robins know when to give up?

This bird is either the most ignorant member of the aviary kingdom or the noblest. I find myself wanting to protect her from making mistakes, but I would probably mess things up by interfering in her preparations. For now, we'll keep watching and waiting for the final outcome. The robin's cheerful chatterings will remind us of her work and fill our home with the awakening of springtime until then. This is God's gift to me.

The wise man built his house upon the rock,
The wise man built his house upon the rock,
The wise man built his house upon the rock,
And the rain came tumbling down.

The rains came down and the floods came up,
The rains came down and the floods came up,
The rains came down and the floods came up,
And the wise man's house stood *firm!*

The foolish man built his house upon the sand,
The foolish man built his house upon the sand,
The foolish man built his house upon the sand,
And the rains came tumbling down.

The rains came down and the floods came up,
The rains came down and the floods came up,

The rains came down and the floods came up,
And the foolish man's house went *down!*[1]

The children were obviously full of delight as
they acted out their latest Sunday school song.
They especially enjoyed making the rains come
down and floods go back up by waving and
shaking their little arms toward the floor, then
reaching *way* up high above their heads. At the
end of the first chorus, they would make their
closed hands slam down on their open palms as
tiny fists signified what it means to stand firm. At
the end of the last chorus—look out! Down
would go the foolish man's house as the kids
would fall giggling to the floor.

Singing with children is a therapeutic
experience. Their joy is all up-front, barely hiding
beneath the surface, waiting to bubble forth at a
moment's notice. "Teacher, teacher, can we sing
'Zaccheus' again? "Watch me tumble, teacher!"
"Let's do 'Jesus Loves Me' now, please, please,
please. . . ."

Every once in a while, the voices of parents
worshiping in pews on the floor above would
filter down to the junior congregation. With a
stately tone, the organ's resounding bass notes
would vibrate the ceiling tiles and fill the
children with awe. The choir's multilayered
hymns somberly reminded each of the youths of
yet to be shared sacraments and other privileges
of Christian adulthood. *Is that what being holy
means, teacher—singing big songs in front of
stained glass windows?*

Years later, I found myself unimpressed with
being all grown-up and singing the very same
hymns that had once sounded so thrilling as I
listened to them echoing against our church's

basement walls. With the mystery solved, the majesty was gone. Would I ever find such joy again, that freedom to tumble and giggle and dance and clap in appreciation that Jesus loved me? Was I really supposed to be able to sit still while praising God?

In the summer of 1971, we arrived at the Timbrooks' farm after driving for two days straight following a brief vacation in northern Ontario. Dave and I had been so far north that the sun didn't completely go down where we chose to camp in late June. Trying to shed a year's worth of heartache and misunderstandings, alone in our tent at night, I would lay close to my husband and watch the twilight filter through the canvas, quietly hoping for a miracle to save our relationship. The trip was a last-ditch effort to salvage what remained of our love for one another; we literally had nowhere to go and no immediate plans for our future. Thinking that being close to nature would help mend our wounds, what we encountered instead were days filled with silence.

Suddenly we both acknowledged our need for fellowship with other human beings. Traveling steadily southward, we made our way down to Lake Superior, around to Thunder Bay, and hit Duluth at daybreak early one morning. Within several hours, we found ourselves at a friend's farm in Iron River, Michigan, which lies close to the Wisconsin border. Drawn by an invitation given to us many months before by one of Dave's ex-neighbors, we arrived unannounced in the middle of a prayer meeting being held in a restored chicken coop next to the barn. Both of us wondered what we were getting ourselves into.

For one thing, I had never been to a gathering

of believers where everyone prayed at the same
time, out loud, in their own words. Initially, it
seemed to me that our friends were attempting to
conjure up some sort of self-manufactured
religious fervor by their behavior. But as they
prayed, my heart began melting as I sensed the
presence of God. A meeting with the Lord in a
chicken coop? Stranger things had been said
to happen to those who have followed Jesus
Christ . . .

My upbringing urged me to be wary of these
people. I felt torn in two directions, between
wanting to jump in my car and head for home,
and feeling the desire to draw closer to God. I
began praying, silently of course, but praying
nonetheless. We ended up staying.

Later that evening, about twenty people
climbed into a school bus owned by the
Timbrooks that had been painted dark green, with
Scripture verses printed in white all over its sides.
Nancy Timbrook was the mother of twelve
children, a woman in her forties who had been a
high school teacher in southeastern Michigan
until she was harassed out of the school district in
the late sixties. Her crime? Teaching students the
real meaning of the big "F word" after a group of
"White Panthers" distributed obscene leaflets on
the school grounds. Due to her attempt to explain
how this word demeans the sacredness and beauty
of human sexuality, a public furor resulted. Nancy
ended up on the religion page of *Time* magazine,
which showed her holding a Bible in the photo
that ran with the article. Needless to say, she was
a woman of strong convictions.

After resigning, Nancy and her family packed
up their children and headed for a timber farm in
Michigan's Upper Peninsula. More than a few
of Nancy's youthful supporters tagged along,

commiting themselves to her attempt to become self-sufficient by living off the land. It was one of the young men who had joined this endeavor who had invited us to stop by the Timbrooks' farm if we were ever in the area.

It's funny how a married couple who have barely been able to speak to one another can instantly feel compelled to stick together in challenging situations. Neither of us wanted to ride in some Jesus freak's crazy-looking school bus to a tent crusade in Hicksville, Wisconsin. But there we were, caught in the midst of a momentum neither of us knew how to grace-fully duck out of. Happily, our marriage has never been the same since. Our decision to go along for the ride ended up changing our lives forever.

Something wonderful started happening to me during our half-hour trip to the revival meeting: I began feeling *younger*. Now, since I was only eighteen and a half, it's not that I was that old to begin with; but I was *old* in terms of feeling weighed down, heavy-hearted, unspontaneous, worldly, and uptight around other people. In other words, I'd forgotten how it felt to be childlike.

For the first time since doing those action songs in Sunday school or sitting around the campfire in Girl Scouts singing "Kum-ba-yah," I encountered the joy of forgetting about myself and yielding to the jubilation of the Holy Spririt. Even Lake Nipigon in northern Canada had failed to induce such an exultant feeling in my heart! But as I sang dozens of old-time gospel choruses, clapping my hands and singing praises out to God with my fellow travelers, I knew that I never wanted to be apart from my Creator again. On that bus ride, I discovered how much I wanted to be my Father's child once more, and was willing to learn how to live in His household no matter what it cost.

Sixteen years have passed since that remarkable evening, which ended up with Dave and I rededicating our lives to the Lord. I continue to enjoy singing and praising my Father more than ever, not in ornate cathedrals or elaborate sanctuaries, but in the everyday moments of my life. Worshiping God always lifts me out of myself and into the Lord's presence in spite of where I am or what I may be doing.

When my babies were fussy or my children have been feverish, I've sung them Psalms and glorified Jesus. Children have a special way of responding to such music. The eighth Psalm even tells us that God has ordained praise from the lips of children and nursing infants. It's only natural that spiritual songs and lullabies are universally appreciated by all of the Lord's little ones.

Therefore, it has been my privilege to minister to my children while praising God. On car trips and on airplanes, in waiting rooms and in rocking chairs, at hotels and at bedsides, I have sung sweetly to my children. With gentle melodies, I have relieved their fears and eased their slumber while expressing my love to them and to their Savior. I've found that I don't need a pipe organ or a hymnal to be close to my Heavenly Father. He is always there, waiting to inhabit my praises, whether I'm ready for Him or not, and the comfort of His Spirit is never far behind.

I love You, Lord, and I lift my voice,
To worship You, O my soul, rejoice!
Take joy my King in what You hear
Let me be a sweet, sweet sound in Your ear.[2]

SIX

Heart
Thoughts

---

*"Niceness"—wholesome, integrated
personality—is an excellent thing. We
must try by every medical, educational,
economic, and political means in our power, to
produce a world where as many people as
possible grow up "nice"; just as we must try to
produce a world where all have plenty to eat.
But we must not suppose that even if we
succeeded in making everyone nice we would
save their souls. A world of nice people, content
in their own niceness, looking no further,
turned away from God, would be just as
desperately in need of salvation as a miserable
world—and might even be more difficult to
save. For mere improvement is no redemption,
though redemption always improves people here
and now and will, in the end, improve them to
a degree we cannot yet imagine. God became
man to turn creatures into sons: not simply to
produce better men of the old kind but to
produce a new kind of man.*[1]

C. S. Lewis

June 20, 1977

I WISH I COULD MAKE HIS SMELL LAST forever in my mind . . . a newborn smell, not like Johnson and Johnson's at all. Forget the baby lotion, powder, and soap—I'll marvel at the wonder of my baby's skin without any products' alterations.

This skin! So soft—blond hairs all over his arms and shoulders, face and ears, soon to disappear. (Later, coarser hair will appear, but I can't even imagine him needing to shave someday!) His downy covering makes me want to preserve its freshness, hair untouched by sweat or seasons.

Every day his eyelashes grow longer. They weren't there at all the first hour. His five-year-old sister noticed it right away: "Look at Baby David's eyes, Mommy. They're bare naked!"

His dark blue eyes see more each day as he watches us smiling and making our funny faces as we ooohhh and aahhh. Content with his quiet attempts at recognition, I'm enjoying his day-to-day progress without pushing ahead. This tiny one will be a grown man soon enough.

Tomorrow? I cannot comprehend it right now; it took so much time just to get him here. Months of waiting, then hours of hard work at the end, followed by anxious moments hoping he would start breathing . . . A full nine months without guarantees, culminating in learning to trust God in new ways as we prayed for the blueness of his skin to vanish with the intake of oxygen. Suddenly he gasped and gulped in a chest full of air at last. We were thankful our son was a strong boy. He looked up at us as if to say, "Of *course* I made it—I'm so glad I'm finally here!" With kisses and shouts of joy we replied, "We're glad you are too. . . ."

This living miracle I hold in my arms took much of us to become himself. And now, as I offer him my breast, I tenderly soothe the impact of our recent separation. I rest easily with him sucking and snuggled up close, reassured by his warmth, his eyes, his sounds—an affirmation of our love held within the gift of his life.

April 3, 1987

David Andrew. It's you! God *did* send you to us . . . I remember it all so vividly. As I look at you now, I realize your time with us is probably half over. Nine years old, nearly ten, you've grown four inches this past year. It's hard for me to believe it.

While watching you in the dentist's chair this afternoon, I was proud of your manly composure. You should have seen your face when you walked into the waiting room to show me your numbed lip. A moment later I wasn't quite sure, but I thought I saw you hesitate for an instant. How you wanted to impress me! But underneath your drooping half-smile, I knew—I knew. It really wasn't as much fun as you thought it was going to be to have your cavity filled.

As usual, I wanted to protect you from feeling any pain. You didn't know it, but I kept peeking in the room to see how you were doing. I prayed you wouldn't be frightened, and wondered if you would make it through okay. Apparently you did just fine. "He was a great patient," Dr. Larson said after she had finished. The receptionist commented on your perfect cooperation. I could tell you were pleased to have fooled them all so well. I wanted to hug you right then and there, but it probably would have helped *me* more than you. You would have been embarrassed!

Not too long ago, you entered the stage when overt displays of my affection aren't exactly welcome, when you want to be recognized for standing on your own two feet. That's all right—I understand. I'll show my concern in other ways and give you the space you need to grow. But whether you know it or not, I'll still be keeping my eye on you and continue to watch you oh so carefully.

When you were little, it wasn't as difficult to know how to express my love for you. You soaked up my attention like a thirsty sponge and spent many days basking in the warmth of my maternal devotion. Goodness, you were easy to please! You smiled so sweetly and spontaneously, a chubby young fellow with dimpled knees and a double chin. Not all babies are as kindhearted as you were. With two older sisters needing much of my energy, it was a blessing to all of us to have you respond so happily to our efforts.

Those same qualities are enabling you to want to be close to Jesus, David. From the first moment of your life, you began hearing about Him: you were birthed into a room filled with prayer. Dad and I wanted you to know right from the very start about your Savior's love and provision for you. Later it seemed the most natural thing in the world for you to want to know more about God's Son. When you asked Him into your heart four years ago, we were so thankful—but not surprised.

You have *always* been drawn to lonely and hurting people. Praying for the needs of others is something you've felt compelled to do for as long as I can remember. We've had many special moments at the dinner table listening to your heartfelt petitions and words of thanks. How many times have you opened your eyes to find us smiling back at you with big grins on our faces?

More than ever, you are entering a time in your life when you will need God's strength and protection. I wish I could shield you from all of the trials and temptations of this upside-down culture we're living in. To be honest with you, I've shed more than a few tears hoping and praying you'll make wise choices.

Strangely enough, your visit to the dentist today reassured me tremendously. You coped *all by yourself* and knew Jesus would help you get through it, didn't you? (Thanks for mentioning your true feelings later and for telling me about your silent plea for help.) We're standing on the threshold of many similar opportunities for growth as you move into the years ahead more independently as a young man who will need to learn how to balance courage with humility. Bit by bit, you'll discover that Dad and I won't always be there in the split seconds when you'll have to decide whether to say yes or no to things that could harm you. It's not just looking both ways before you cross the street that we'll be concerned about anymore.

From the day of your arrival, we knew our love would only be able to carry you so far, imperfect as it is in so many ways. At times we've struggled with knowing how best to care for you, teach you, guide you. Being a parent is a humbling experience. Often it all boils down to trusting God to fill in the gaps left in the wake of even our best efforts to be good examples for you to follow.

Frankly, there are times when we think we could have done a better job. (I can hear you saying "Amen" to that!) We have prayed for wisdom many times . . . and also for a greater measure of patience. On occasion, we've told you we were sorry and asked for your forgiveness for falling short. We've learned a lot from one another, haven't we?

We can be thankful that you and Dad and I are *all* children when it comes to our relationship with the Lord, that *each* of us needs redemption from sin. Isn't it reassuring to know that we have a Father in heaven who will be *eternally* faithful in His love for us? *From the beginning, you've belonged to Him instead of to Dad and me.* Basically you're on temporary loan to our household. The values and goals and dreams we share with you are meant to influence you for a lifetime, but these early years will be very brief compared to what lies ahead. Our time together goes more quickly with each passing season.

In return for the gift of guiding your life, we have given you much of ourselves. More than anything, I think you need us to be "merciful and gracious, slow to anger and abundant in loving kindness and truth."[2] The world outside our doors is harsh enough without you having to face parents who would accuse and criticize and hurt you. No, there is never an excuse for that. I pray that God will continue to remind us of His way of caring for His own precious children when it comes to knowing how to care for ours.

I love you, David, and hope that someday you will look back on your childhood with a peaceful heart. Even though it feels like you'll be here forever, that the mud-tracked floors and misplaced socks will never end, the Lord has other plans for you. You see, the measurement of our "success" as your parents will manifest itself in your ability to grow *beyond* us into a productive life of your own. The beauty and joy of our early *at*tachment is gradually evolving into your eventual *de*tachment from our home. Before you know it, you will be the one making decisions concerning how to express your love for Christ within the world as a coheir with us of His Kingdom. Neither Dad nor I can make those choices for you.

I will try to daily remind myself of the finite nature of my influence in your life, keeping in mind how much a part of one another we will always be. The days we share are more precious than they appear; there is still so much I have left to give you! Please take your time, David . . . You don't need to hurry. The older you get, the more you'll find there is left to know, learn, and discover. Life is an amazing adventure, filled with endless possibilities. I'm glad we're making this journey together!

The future no longer seems as far away as I once imagined it would be. It's easy now to picture you shaving and talking with a different, deeper voice. Your skin has been covered with sweat and dirt on more days than I can count. There isn't an ounce of baby fat left on your string-bean body. Watching you change from the infant I once cradled in my arms into the energetic young man you are today has been astounding.

I'm looking forward to seeing your God-given talents blossom into a fruitful ministry on His behalf. Forgive me for indulging in wishful thinking, but I sometimes wonder: Will you choose to serve Jesus as a pastor or a teacher someday? Or a missionary or writer perhaps? Will you hold tight to the Word of God as the foundational truth that will guide your life? Will you steadfastly refuse to let go of the love you feel for your Lord today so that what has come so naturally for you will never perish or fade away?

May your faith grow brighter and clearer and stronger in the years ahead! For the time being, I will be here to remind you, in as many ways as I can think of, what it means to be a child of the King. Let's continue to praise God for the many good gifts He has given to each of us in the years to come!

And by the way, before I forget to tell you, I'm glad you remembered to brush your teeth tonight. Your appointment with the dentist seems to have worked wonders. After all these years, I don't think you're going to need me to tell you to brush between meals any more.

Creation seems to be delegation through and through. He will do nothing of Himself which can be done by creatures. I suppose that is because He is a giver.[3]

C. S. Lewis

SEVEN

Out of the Cabbage Patch and into the Garbage Pail

---

*F*ROM AN INTERVIEW WITH MOTHER TERESA:

"Some people say that there are too many children in India, and yet you're saving children many of whom would otherwise die."

Yes, many would die, especially among those children who are unwanted. Quite possibly they would have been either thrown away or killed. But that way is not for us; our way is to preserve life, the life of Christ in the life of the child.

"So you wouldn't agree with people who say there are too many children in India."

I do not agree because God always provides. He provides for the flowers and the birds, for every thing in the world that he has created. And those little children are his life. There can never be enough.[1]

My DAUGHTERS BOUGHT THEIR Cabbage Patch Kids in December 1984. At the time, there were so few of the dolls available that stores were holding drawings to award customers the right to buy one of the limited number they had. When my oldest daughter "won" an opportunity to purchase a "Kid" at $39.99, selected out of hundreds of entrants, I broke the bad news: "If you're really serious about getting this, it's one of those things you're going to have to pay for yourself. These toys aren't worth forty dollars, and I want you to think about whether this will be a wise use of your money or not."

Normally that would have been the end of it since Joanna, at twelve years of age, usually didn't have forty dollars available to spend on such stuff—but she had received enough Christmas money from relatives to cover the expense. "That's what the money's for, Mom," she explained as she decided to go ahead and get the doll, named "Cedric." Soon afterwards, Katy was also able to find a Cabbage Patch Kid to buy, and our family ended up adopting two of the ugliest-looking pretend playmates I had ever laid my eyes on. (So much for the exquisitely crafted Madame Alexander babies who had lived with us up until that time.)

Rather than claiming to have origins similar to real babies, the "Kids" had birth certificates certifying their delivery in cabbage patches. They appeared bloated, puffy, with distorted features, like caricatures of Spanky on "Our Gang." They were treated like baby dolls, but weren't *real* baby dolls, if you know what I mean, and I still believed they had been incredibly overpriced. Yet another American dreamer had discovered a fantastic way to make a bundle of money by exploiting the imagination of children. In inventing a new twist to the art of make-believe mothering, some modern-day wizard had created a unique species of creatures and convinced millions of youngsters that they just *had* to have a Cabbage Patch doll. Even Nancy Reagan was photographed giving the dolls away to the needy that memorable Christmas.

Needless to say, I was unhappy that my children had succumbed to some guy's get-rich-quick scheme, yet was unable to articulate my reservations about his product line until later. In the meantime, the girls had a great deal of fun with their toys and I got used to having the "Kids" around. I even forget about how much they had cost and how gross they had looked to me initially.

In the summer of 1986, my nine-year-old son David asked me to drive him to a drugstore one afternoon so he could buy a special type of bubble gum card. Explaining that he had saved up two dollars for this purpose, he told me several of his best friends were starting vast collections of these new items. When we entered the store, I glanced at the wrappers as he picked out nine packets and assumed they were Cabbage Patch Kid cards, since that's what appeared to be on the cover. David was elated. He finally had obtained something his buddies had been raving about for weeks.

Later that day, I noticed some of his cards lying on the dining room table, discovering that they were a takeoff on the Cabbage Patch Kids image called *Garbage Pail Kids*. I soon found that pandering to America's affluent youth had sunk to an all-time low. I was profoundly dismayed and deeply shocked by what I saw. Here's a sampling of the forty-five-card collection my son had

bought with his money earlier in the day, all
depictions of Cabbage Patch Kids "in serious
trouble":

Warmin' Norman, #161, B Series: A cowboy
Kid pierced with five arrows, wearing a
weird grin while being burned at the stake
by Indians.

Mauled Paul, #15, B Series: A baby Kid
hobbling around on a crutch, painfully
wandering in a daze, with two black eyes, a
bloody nose, and seven roughly stitched
lacerations.

Fryin' Brian, #4, A Series: A convicted Kid
being executed in an electric chair, while
helplessly convulsing from the current
shooting through his body.

Meltin' Melissa, #28, A Series: A black Kid
shown as a candle, with her lighted wick
causing her head to melt, wax dripping all
over her body and her left eye oozing out of
its socket.

Frigid Brigid, #32, A Series: A gray female
Kid solidly frozen in a chunk of ice, replete
with icicles hanging from her forehead.

Stormy Heather, #7, A Series: A young
schoolgirl Kid being split in two as she is
struck by lightning on her way to school.

Art Apart, no number: A young Kid propped
up against a wall in shock, with his arms and
legs lying on the floor nearby after having
been torn off.

On the backs of the cards were various "awards" and "licenses" addressed to the card's owner, with a space to fill in the child's name. I've listed a few excerpts here after each title:

> *Big Stink Award:* "Sure, other kids smell worse than you—but they're all six feet under!"

> *Clumsy Award:* "The safest place for you might be a padded cell—have a nice trip!"

> *Juvenile Delinquency Award:* "You will reach the top—you'll become public enemy number one!"

> *Bully License:* "This license permits you to follow your natural calling—namely picking on people smaller than you. You can beat up, intimidate, cheat, lie, and extort to your heart's content."

Finding it difficult to believe anyone would make such hideous products for young children, I immediately called both David and his younger brother Jon into my room to discuss the cards. Not wanting to simply demand that the boys destroy them, I decided to take a different approach, hoping to teach my sons how to evaluate the message of the cards for themselves.

"Boy, David. These cards are pretty wild. Have you looked closely at any of them yet?"

"All my friends are collecting them, Mom. Jeff has over a hundred. What's wrong?" He could tell I wasn't pleased. I knew that neither Jon nor David had really examined the scenes on the cards. Picking a few of them up, I handed several to each boy.

"Well, I was surprised to see what's going on in these pictures, honey. Can you describe what's happening in this one for me? Jon, how about telling me about the one showing the Cabbage Patch Kid with all the nails pounded into him?"

How I would have preferred to have banished the cards myself and to forbid my children to ever look at another one again! It broke my heart to have to point out the scenes that were portrayed. But because I knew they were the latest fad and even kindergarteners Jon's age were collecting them, it was clear that my sons had to form their own opinions, with a little help from Mom.

I'll never forget my boys' reactions as they thoughtfully inspected the cards very carefully, one after another. As soon as they were done, they knew, just as their mother had, what needed to be done. It was a sad lesson for them to be learning at such young ages, but neither of them have ever asked to buy or borrow any cards since. David told me yesterday his friend now has 357 of them, and he's told my son he thinks they'll be worth a lot of money someday. As for David and Jon, I have overheard them on occasion trying to warn their friends about the sad condition of the Garbage Pail Kids and about adults who would manufacture scenes depicting such cruelty towards children.

Children. Gifts of God worthy of our protection, or things we throw away when conceived inconveniently? Human life. An expression of our Creator's love, made in His image, to be welcomed with joy and compassion regardless of a baby's genetic condition, or simply a "higher life-form" to be torn apart in the womb or starved after birth if determined to be unacceptable to society? You and I. Mothers whose hearts are breaking over the destruction of those too young or helpless to speak for themselves, or women claiming to respect the right of others to make choices associated with the dehumanization and deathmaking of children?

The little girl came into the room with an armful of toys, once again prepared to sit for an hour and watch Mommy go through her exercise routine in aerobics class. But as her mother danced, the toys were left in their appropriate corner, where Rita had gently placed them. The three-year-old's eyes steadily followed the active body of her mother back and forth as it moved across the room with increasing momentum. An abused child who had been placed in the Martin family's foster care home, Rita had recently been adopted by them, with the official papers having been signed several months ago.

Suddenly, up jumped the girl, leaping to her feet in one quick motion. She began to move slowly and hesitantly at first, while focusing on the form of her mother.

"Right, two, three, kick; now left, two, three, Grapevine! Forward, two, three, and back, two, three, again!" With an awkward rhythm, Rita tried to match Mommy's steps at the back of the room. A determined look, mixed with excitement, covered her small face as she kept her attention fixed on her mother. The look said: *I am going to do it just like you, Mommy. I can be a dancer, too!*

As I continued to watch little Rita dance alongside her rapidly moving mama, graceful as any child of that age could ever hope to be, I thought: *Yes, darling Rita, keep watching*

Mommy, and someday you will be just like your mother too.

Children's dreams and child's play: reflections of their surroundings and the shaping of their futures. Thinking of walking up and down the aisles of toys, eyes wide open, I wonder: What will my son play with today? Green slime and fanged-toothed monsters? Or will he sit right here beside me as I type these words, drawing with bright colored pencils, filling in the outward pictures of his mind? Will he imagine hordes of superheroes battling demons and dragons—robot/people/cars chasing one another down flaming highways and deserted cityscapes? Or scenes from nature he remembers from the walk we took in the park yesterday? *I will help him choose. . . .*

As Jonathan thinks and plays, putting his imagination to work, all the while he is growing into the person he will one day become, absorbing the values of his surroundings and those around him. He listens so intently to what I have to say. His big, beautiful, trusting eyes miss nothing that I do.

I will be your teacher, Jonathan, my precious son. I love you.

"The life of Christ in the life of the child . . . little children are his life."

From God's own hand instead of a cabbage patch, and not headed for a garbage pail.

I think this is something we all have to understand: that love begins at home. In our day we see with growing clarity that the sorrows of the world have their origin in the family. . . . Where is the unborn child? Dead!

Why? Because we do not want him. . . . One day, however, we will have to meet the Lord of the universe. What will we tell him about that child, about the old father or mother? They are his creatures, children of God. What will be our answer?[2]

Mother Teresa

EIGHT

Unsung Heroes

*The desire of men to claim their children
may be the crucial impulse of civilized life.
It is chiefly in the nuclear household that the
man's connection to his children becomes
indispensable. He is the key provider. His
fatherhood is direct and unimpeachable, and he
identifies, loves, and provides for his offspring
. . . the crucial difference between a civilized
and an uncivilized society is the attitude of
males toward their children.*[1]

George Gilder

*H*E RIDES TO WORK IN A FORD station wagon
instead of a Nissan 300ZX, dressed in a well-
worn suit purchased at a clearance sale, with a
sack lunch carried along to cut down on
"optional" expenses. After working a hectic nine
hours directing the state's Office of Mental
Retardation, he quickly returns home and is
immediately surrounded by two young sons, a
couple of adolescent daughters, and an eleven-
week-old puppy. "Dad's home!" calls out one of
the girls in a signal that announces his timely
arrival. "When do we eat?"

On most nights, for the remainder of his evening this dedicated dad will invest what is left of his time and energy in the lives of his wife and children.

Who is this unique guy who has yet to own a set of decent stereo components or belong to the local health club? His colleagues often wonder why he chooses to head for home rather than join them at a trendy bar after finishing work for the day; they smile condescendingly whenever his family cruises in to say hello and gives him hugs. Blaming his lack of social astuteness on his "religious orientation," I imagine they must pity him for the sacrifices he must make to support our larger-than-average family.

Like other men who are being transformed by God's love, my husband is one of the unsung heroes of his generation, a courageous rebel who refuses to bow to the latest assortment of man-made idols. For his stubborn refusal to follow the pack and his conscious choice to become the head of a "traditional" family, he is rewarded with stacks of bills, interrupted sleep, and arbitration duties in sibling disputes. But that's not all—this liberated man, like many other husbands and fathers around the nation, has found real satisfaction in fulfilling his God-given role as the servant-leader of his family in spite of the many sacrifices he makes. Our children and I will be forever grateful for his presence in our lives.

The women's movement warned me to be on my guard against this person who would attempt to deny me my rights by placing me under his authority. A sexist tyrant? Hardly! When I look into his eyes, I see only love and concern for my well-being. Male chauvinist? No, not at all. When we openly share our concerns and work through our disagreements, it always comes back to our

responsibilities and commitment to *one another.*
Two individuals who have lost their autonomy and
surrendered their sexual freedom by obtaining a
marriage license? Now *that's* the most hilarious
accusation of all! We care about each other to
such an extent that we don't *want* to fool around
with anyone else!

We are two who have become one by being
shaped, molded, and pressed together throughout
seventeen years of living out our vows to one
another. I have never forgotten his solemn answer
of "I will" in response to the following passage
from the *Book of Common Prayer,* nor the sacred
pledge he earnestly repeated afterwards:

> Wilt thou love her, comfort her, honour, and
> keep her in sickness and in health; and,
> forsaking all others, keep thee only to her, so
> long as ye both shall live?
>
> . . . to have and to hold from this day
> forward, for better for worse, for richer for
> poorer, in sickness and in health, to love and
> to cherish, till death us do part, according to
> God's holy ordinance; and thereto I plight
> thee my troth.

What a day that was! Like most couples,
neither of us had any idea of what we were *really*
getting ourselves into! Learning to live "as one"
isn't easy or natural for *anybody!*

Building a home in which a family can bloom
and thrive involves hard work—plenty of it—on
both sides. While some might say I was just
"lucky" to find a young man who would take his
marriage seriously, I must be perfectly honest and
say that there have been literally dozens
(hundreds?) of times when we were ready to

throw in the towel during the first ten years.

Slowly but surely, obedience to following God's design for our lives has enabled us to yield ourselves more completely to the power of the Holy Spirit, which has supernaturally changed us from the inside out. No human counselor would have had the ability to teach us how to love and serve one another or conform to Biblical standards for marriage. But what would have been impossible for the two of us has been *triumphantly* possible through Christ Jesus our Lord!

Each day I find myself faced with an important set of decisions regarding my marriage, no matter how much work needs to be done, what the children are up to, or whoever else might need me: I must *daily* choose to say *yes* to opening up my heart to the Lord and reading His Word; to being available to my husband and to preparing my heart for his homecoming at the end of what has usually been an exhausting day for both of us. Even when significant problems arise or if I've reached my stress limit, this man who gives so much of himself to serve our family *deserves to be loved, appreciated, and respected.* Through honoring the gifts of his labor and provision to us, it is my sincere hope that the burden he carries on our behalf will feel at least a little bit lighter and that his spirit will be renewed through the bond we all share.

One of the best pieces of marital advice I've heard came from a friend who was born in New Zealand and has lived all over the world. It's obvious that she comes from a nurturing family because of her own capacity for nurturing others. When I asked her if her parents were as kind and capable with their twelve children as she is with her six, my friend replied, "Oh, at *least!*" She then began to talk about her parents at length and shared something I'll never forget: "Deb, I can remember my mother *always* taking the time to run a brush through her hair, put a little makeup on, and change into clean clothes before my dad got home—and all this in spite of having twelve kids underfoot!"

Superwoman? Saint? Subservient housewife? No—merely an ordinary woman who understood the significance of a loving gesture made in the midst of crazy days filled with more than their share of work and hassle. *Such actions spring from a commitment to bring beauty and love into even the most mundane or challenging circumstances, and nourish a marriage in powerful ways as a result.*

Sometimes I find myself wondering what our lives would have been like if we had remained childless or had waited longer than eighteen months after getting married to start our family. I always end up with exactly the same conclusion, however! Becoming a father has changed Dave in as many ways as becoming a mother has changed me, and *these changes have all been for the better.*

Parenthood has drastically altered the way we operate in the world while deepening our capacity to give and receive love. The same strong arms that have held me in the privacy of our bed became the arms that faithfully supported me during the births of our children; the nights of lost sleep and the stress of living through times of injury and illness have taught us to lose ourselves for the sake of caring for those nearest and dearest to us. What meaningful times we have shared! Right along with the painful experiences and upsetting events has come an overflowing of

God's grace and peace. While the past fifteen
years have been far from comfortable, they have
been exceedingly fruitful and have produced
everlasting results in our lives.

I have especially enjoyed watching the
Fatherhood of God express itself through my
husband. For example, he knows how to be both
tender and stern with our sons and daughters.
When I have seen him lay his hands on a feverish
brow or a pulled muscle, I have become a witness
to the paradox of granite-like humility. When
Dave's voice pronounces, "Bedtime!" it carries a
sense of urgency and authority I have never been
able to come *close* to. Like E. F. Hutton, when
Dad speaks, our kids listen.

Being a father allows a man to wake up to his
capacity for leadership and accountability to God
in ways that no amount of formal schooling can
accomplish. This rigorous, on-the-job training
forces men to finally abandon boyhood, unlike
most careers that can bring only *self*-satisfaction as
men attempt to "make something" of *themselves.*"
Fatherhood brings about *death* to self in so *many*
wonderful ways! Consequently, it makes much
more sense when engaged in from an eternal
perspective.

So let's hear it for the men on the front lines
who battle the stereotypes of Magnum, P.I. and
Archie Bunker; who, unlike Bill Cosby, are far
from being famous fathers or multitalented
millionaires; and whose spiritual strength makes
Arnold Schwarznegger seem like a ninety-eight-
pound weakling. These men of God who are
unafraid to assume the headship of their families
deserve our highest praise. Where would we be
without them? Where would they be without *us?*
We need one another *more than ever* in this
postindustrial age of "enlightenment," to

demonstrate before a watching world that fatherhood, as well as motherhood, *matters.*

The reason why our childhoods were one enthusiasm after another was that we hadn't yet found an organizing center for our lives and a goal that would demand our all and our best. The Christian faith is the discovery of that center in the righteous God. Christian discipleship is a decision to walk in his ways, steadily and firmly, and then finding that the way integrates all our interests, passions and gifts, our human needs and our eternal aspirations. It is the way of life we were created for. There are endless challenges in it to keep us on the growing edge of faith; there is always a righteous God with us to make it possible for us to persevere.[2]

Eugene H. Peterson

NINE

Stranded
But Never
Alone

*P*arents of today are faced with the greatest
tasks that have ever been asked of any
generation. They are asked to be solely
responsible for developing the coming
generation without the help of extended
families, without the help of concerned
neighbors, and without the help of the
community. They are being bombarded with
"how-to" advice from the experts, and they are
constantly being judged by teachers, doctors,
and psychologists on how they are performing.
On top of that, mothers are being asked not
only to mother but to be an equal part of the
earning power of the modern family. Is it any
wonder that parents are overwhelmed with the
tasks of parenting?[1]

Dr. Donna Ewy

I SIT TODAY IN FRONT OF MY TYPEWRITER, surrounded
by four blocks' worth of empty houses. It
seems I'm the only mother home this morning, or

for that matter on most weekday mornings like this one. By 8 A.M. I'm usually stranded right in the middle of my own neighborhood. Any women close to my age who live nearby have normally left for work by this time, and those with children have them tucked away in school or day care by now. It sure gets quiet around here during the day.

My only social contacts consist of brief hellos from the mail carrier and occasional waves to retired folks as they wind their way up the street to Russ's IGA. When hanging the laundry up to dry, I'm accompanied by the sound of a blue jay's chirrup or one of the city buses that roll by our door every half-hour. If my youngest son Jon and I decide to go for a hike, we rarely have our privacy disturbed by passers-by. The world I remember from my childhood, filled with dozens of neighborhood playmates with their mothers busy at home, is far different from the experiences of my own children. When they have wanted to play with friends, I've had to drive them for the most part. Kids *their* ages aren't home during the day either.

As for my extended family, the closest members live seven hundred and fifty miles away. If my relatives did live in our area, I wouldn't see them very often since most of them are gone for much of the day, too. My grandma's the only one I can think of who, at age eighty-nine, is now home most of the time, but she lives in Florida. I've seen her only once in the last six years.

The effects of my societally imposed isolation can be broken down into two parts: good days and bad days. On good days, I feel productive, energetic, and thankful for my relative independence and the opportunities it affords me with my children. On bad days, I'm likely to complain a lot, shed tears of weariness, and yes, even yell at my kids. Frankly, most moms who find themselves in similar situations feel overwhelmed at times. I'm no exception. We're a high-risk group for depression, substance abuse, obesity, and burnout. Even the best of us have bad days, and being abandoned by the rest of society doesn't help *any* of us.

Very few mothers get more than a token amount of help from people outside their immediate families. That's a precarious position for women with so many responsibilities. Fortunately, the majority of us do amazingly well given the current status of our role, but a small percentage tragically end up in jail or psychiatric wards for their inability to cope, victims of a dehumanizing value system that places higher worth on the prestige of paychecks and job titles than on labors of love. Our collective failure as a society to provide resources, esteem, and companionship to mothers at home is a national embarrassment. No, it's more than that—it's a travesty.

In 1970, a poll of nearly one thousand women found a whopping 52 percent of its respondents claiming that the most enjoyable aspect of being a woman for them was motherhood. In second place, at 22 percent, was being a wife. Personal rights and freedom came in third, at 14 percent, and in last place, careers, at 9 percent. A nearly identical poll conducted in 1983 points to the tremendous impact of the feminist movement on mothering. The results? Rights and freedom jumped in popularity, from 14 to 32 percent, assuming the top position as "most enjoyable." Career and motherhood tied for second. In the 1983 poll, 26 percent of the respondents said their careers brought them the most satisfaction, nearly *three times* as many as in 1970. The figure

for motherhood had been cut in half. More
significantly, the least important aspect of being a
woman to the later poll's participants was being a
wife, which came in a distant last. Down from
second place (22 percent) in 1970, the figure for
1983 was *6 percent,* a reduction of nearly three-
quarters. These shifts represent one of the most
revolutionary changes in women's ideas about
marriage and family life that has ever occurred in
all of history.[2]

Given the scope of these trends, those of us
who have continued to highly value our roles as
wives and mothers are an endangered minority.
The worth of our work has been eclipsed by the
opinion-shapers on Madison Avenue and Wall
Street, proving that one can never underestimate
the power of advertising executives and the
almighty dollar. Private enterprise gains much
from the earnings of working women compared to
coupon-clipping, budget-conscious, stay-at-home
moms. Needing a second car in order to get to
work? That suits Ford Motors or Toyota just fine,
ladies. And how about dining out more often
because there's little time left to cook dinner after
getting home at 5? Great! Most restaurants,
planning on your arrival, offer special prices on
kids' meals to make it easier for you. A better
wardrobe? Improved image? Step right up to your
closest department store, which counts on your
regular patronage. Few families want to give up a
second income, considering all of the possible
amenities now available to the modern American
family. And all along, women thought their
opinions were actually being shaped by people
like Betty Friedan and Gloria Steinem!

For those of us who have resisted the pressure
to relinquish our beliefs about marriage and the
family, what has caused us to remain committed to

a dying ideal? Why aren't we willing to just up and leave our neighborhoods like everyone else? What is keeping us so close to home? Ignorance? Laziness? Our husband's salaries? Fear of the "real" world? Hardly! For most of us, I suggest, it is due to the fact that we accept *a different value system*. Simply put, our husbands and our children are the most important people in our lives, and we refuse to compromise their well-being (and our own) by exhausting ourselves for the sake of money or an "enlarged" identity. We invest ourselves in a way of life that we believe promotes the health of our families and, ultimately, the health of our society as well. We'll continue to make this investment regardless of the price tag others place on our efforts. In other words, we have chosen to follow our hearts rather than respond to a materialistic view of the value of human life.

As for me, I consider myself blessed. I've come to view the world from a vantage-point far removed from the underlying philosophies of our dominant culture as expressed in magazines such as *Self, Ms.,* and *Cosmopolitan.* Like Thoreau, my outlook has been transformed by drawing away from the pressures of cultural conformity and taking the time to look from the outside in. Seclusion works wonders for the soul.

What some women equate with bondage, I have found offers liberation: I have been free to answer my children's cries and questions and pleas for attention; to sit for hours on end contemplating the meaning of life while rocking my babies to sleep and building Lego castles and watching my kids splash in the tub; to make deep and lasting friendships with remarkable women at my kitchen table over tea, while strolling along beaches or picnicking at local parks. I've chosen to let others discover the tyranny of competition, assignment deadlines, disagreeable bosses, and inflexible hours. As Bob Dylan's lyrics expressed it, "we've all gotta serve somebody," and I've preferred to serve God by serving the people I love.

By not "having it all," I've settled for something infinitely more precious than paychecks. I've become the guardian of new life, a builder of memories, a source of inspiration, and a central figure in my family's history. *What I have contributed to their lives is invaluable and irreplaceable.*

The sheer quantity of time I've spent on these endeavors is astronomical. People-making doesn't happen overnight or just in the evenings and on weekends. To those who say it's only "quality" that counts, I suggest trying the quality-time approach with their garden. As anyone who's ever had one knows, a garden requires a lot of work.* What counts is *being there,* my friends, through thick and thin. Nobody, and I mean nobody, can pay someone to do what only a mother will do for free. You can't *buy* that kind of nurturing, protection, and interaction on a twenty-four-hour, seven-days-a-week basis.

It's got to be awfully confusing to young children when Mommy or Daddy only bother to stay home on sick days and snow days. What does this kind of parenting say to a child? You're only worth my care when you're ill or if the weather

*It must be cultivated, planted, watered, weeded, harvested. A certain fixed amount of time is required to do these things properly. With gardening, it's not so much a question of making the most of every moment. Rather, it's a question of making sure *enough* time is spent. How much more do our children, who are worth infinitely more than plants, deserve *sufficient* time spent with them by us?

happens to be lousy? Kids are smarter than that. They realize that "where your treasure is, there shall your heart be also." When staying at her grandmother's recently while her mom was out of town on work-related business, the five-year-old daughter of a close friend of mine put it this way: "Grandma, Mommy didn't *have* to go, she *wanted* to go." With tears in her eyes, this wise little girl had summed up her situation perfectly.

This isn't to say I haven't thought about spending a weekend in New York or have never envied my husband as he would leave for a day away from three sick children, a messy house, or a huge pile of dirty clothes. There is *plenty* of discouraging work to be done behind the scenes in the life of a family, lots of imperfections that grate on one's nerves, days when one dreams of draining the bank account and taking off for sunny Florida. Alone.

With each new family member, the amount of work to do seems to multiply almost exponentially—especially the laundry. Gracious dining becomes a thing of the past with a baby at one's breast, a toddler dribbling food all over himself and his high chair, and a preschooler spelling a wide assortment of interesting words all over the tablecloth with her alphabet soup. Thankless tasks, hundreds of them, make up a significant amount of the time and effort mothering requires. It isn't unusual to occasionally fantasize about how much easier it would be to just be gone for the day.

I must confess that I've prayed more than my fair share of prayers for deliverance, calling out in desperation, "Dear Lord, deliver me from poopy diapers and stubborn stains and otitis media! Protect Thy servant's mind from the effects of phone solicitors, scattered Play Doh bits, and

Mister Rogers! Heavenly Father, give me patience
to face yet another whining child/pile of
washing/broken vacuum cleaner . . . and please
remind me once more why I decided to be here
in the first place. . . ."

At times such as these, I am thankful that we
are not home alone in the universe. There *is*
someone who cares, who closely identifies with
feelings of loneliness and isolation, who
experienced what it means to surrender
everything for the sake of love. His words have
meant nothing less than my survival as I have
pondered them in my heart while performing the
myriad tasks required of my role:

> Come to me, all you who are weary and
> burdened, and I will give you rest. Take my
> yoke upon you and learn from me, for I am
> gentle and humble in heart, and you will
> find rest for your souls. For *my* yoke is easy
> and my burden is light.

Yes, this gentle teacher and humble servant has
asked me to put love into action, to lose my life
if I want to really find it. In the midst of my
frustrations, the words of Jesus have reminded me
that what I do is *ministry*, not drudgery, and that
my actions are an offering to the Lord Himself. It
is clear that my Creator values the very kinds of
service the world scorns. The work my society
ridicules God counts as crucial to the health of
my soul.

In looking back over my years as a mother, I
see the wisdom of Christ's teachings. The choices
I have made have kept me on a steady (though
sometimes faltering) pilgrimage, causing me to
hunger for the presence of God on days when the
loneliness of my vocation threatened to paralyze

me. Although often painful initially, the sacrifices of mothering have helped me become a less selfish, more tolerant person. I've been forced to call upon God when I've felt inadequate and to ask His forgiveness when I've fallen short. In return, I've been given priceless gifts of hope and joy and peace instead of financial remuneration. Although attractively seductive in appearance, money and power can *never* give lasting happiness, spiritual maturity, or eternal life. Yet being a mother has placed me on the road to obtaining *all* of these things. Ironic, isn't it?

It's all according to one's point of view, it seems. From where I sit today, looking out my windows at all those empty houses, I know where I would rather be any day.

> Don't let the world around you squeeze you into its mould, but let God re-make you so that your whole attitude of mind is changed. Thus you will prove in practice that the will of God's good, acceptable to him and perfect.[3]

TEN

A Circle of Caring

Now that the majority of American families live in nuclear families, we are ever aware of our own isolation and of how nice it is to have others involved with our babies and children in more than a perfunctory way. We are learning, often the hard way, how vital it is to have others around who care and who willingly give help when needed. Not that we wish to go backward and give up our independent family. It's a matter of how to have one's apartness without losing necessary and intense human contact.[1]

Dr. Dana Raphael

SUSAN . . . PHYLLIS . . . JUDY . . . Joan . . . Linda . . . Ellen . . . Traci . . . Lori . . . Annie . . . Barb . . . Christy . . . Shawn—twelve women, twelve labors, all vividly etched in my mind as I remember their fatigue and courage, their tears and smiles as they worked to birth their babies. Giving birth is rarely easy, and when the going gets rough, the journey is aided by the assistance of friends. These mothers, and all of the others I have had the privilege of teaching and sharing

with, have shaped my life in many ways. Above
all, I have learned that motherhood *needs*
company. Each pregnancy, each birth, and each
baby have a character of their own. Even women
who have been through it all many times before
benefit from the companionship of other mothers.

I feel very strongly that *all* mothers find their
identity strengthened and renewed when they are
supported by caring and empathetic women.
While each woman has to find her own way of
doing things and developing her individuality as a
mother, it never hurts to talk to and be around
women involved in similar tasks. Because our
culture no longer provides for this need, each
woman must construct her own support network
of friends and family to encourage her in her
motherhood role. A recent study, in fact, found
that women who lacked this support network ran
a significantly higher risk of postpartum, or after
birth, depression.[2] The researchers recommended
that childbearing women be encouraged to find
ways of filling the gap that currently exists in the
care of mothers after they return home from the
hospital or birthing center, or immediately after
birth when their babies are born at home.

Since becoming a childbirth educator and
breastfeeding counselor in the midseventies, I
have tried to do my part. Many women all over
the country, like myself, have become mothers'
advocates in an effort to compensate for the
dreadful lack of recognition and support for
women entering motherhood. At times the
emphasis on a medical approach to childbearing
and lactation threatens to overwhelm us. These
events, unlike pathological diseases, are a very
real and substantial part of the experience of
healthy mothers, involving not only their bodies,
but their minds, their spirits, their histories, and

their families as well. When an integral part of a
woman's sexuality is redefined as a medically-
oriented event requiring expert care and the
supervision of obstetrical surgeons, childbearing
ends up becoming dehumanized and frightening,
as well as seeming to be abnormally dangerous to
both mother and child.

I have a difficult time believing, for instance,
that our Maker originally intended 23 percent of
all babies to be born by Cesarean section. That is
the current rate nationally, up from just a little
more than 4 percent in 1970. This trend, and
many others as well, I find deeply disturbing. My
way of dealing with it is to fight back with love
and concern and compassion instead of hard data.
(Perhaps I should stick to the plain facts and let
them speak for themselves!) I honestly believe
that healthy childbearing women are often better
served and better cared for by midwives.

When I was pregnant with our fourth child,
Jonathan, I became involved in a controversy with
a group of obstetricians who wanted to sponsor
their own childbirth classes instead of referring
couples to the childbirth association I taught
with. The doctors were tired of having couples
ask questions about routine practices such as
I.V.'s, enemas, lying flat for birth with one's legs
up in the air, etc. Although they couldn't fault us
for sharing inaccurate information, they didn't
like us teaching alternatives to their routines or
pointing out the risks associated with them. They
had no use for this information; so the OB's
started their very own Lamaze classes specifically
for their patients in order to teach them the *right*
way to have a baby. Never mind that they required
all of their clients to be strapped to fetal monitors
throughout labor, which have never been proven
to produce better outcomes than what can be

gained by listening to babies' heart tones intermittently with a fetascope—they felt no need to discuss opposing viewpoints. And so what if they routinely administered a synthetic hormone during labor and artificially ruptured the amniotic sac in most cases. Even though studies point to the hazards of *both* of these practices, they didn't think couples ought to know. On point after point the doctors were determined to present a medical view of giving birth while ignoring the purpose and intent of true education for childbirth, which was designed to encourage parents to consider their own needs and preferences to enable them to have a genuinely *family-centered* birth experience. What the physicians wanted taught was a *doctor-centered* view of birth, largely because of their fear of litigation.

The organizations which originally fought for the right of fathers to be in the delivery room attempted to restore birth as an event to be shared by entire families. In other words, advocates of normal birth called for *parent-directed birth assistance* as an alternative to *hospital-oriented labor and delivery.* However, as malpractice issues clouded the horizon, birthing options became limited in many communities. Today professional medical associations continue to attempt to define the terms of birth for millions of American women, while the primary voices which should be shaping birthing practices are being lost.

How will women ever know what it is like to give birth surrounded by caring loved ones instead of masked and gowned health care providers if no one is left to speak up for *normal* birth? How will mothers ever know the satisfaction of being able to completely nourish their infants without supplements of glucose water and/or formula if no one speaks up loudly and clearly on behalf of *normal* lactation? There's still plenty of room for fathers and mothers to represent themselves and their infants. Some battles may have been won, but there are many more issues left to confront. Also, since most hospitals and physicians are in this business to make money, we must not forget that they compete with one another for clients. It has never ceased to amaze me how fast a particular policy changes when the hospital or doctor's group across town alters their rules or routines. Boom! Just like that, outdated practices tend to go out the window.

As women, we need to realize how much we benefit from sharing our talents and resources. We understand things that many highly trained health care providers will *never* understand, and it is up to us to inform them of *our* perspectives. Only mothers know such things as how to internally cooperate with the process of birth or how to relax in a way that causes milk to be let down while nursing a baby, in addition to all of the other mechanisms related to aspects of women's sexuality that are emotionally mediated. These things cannot be clinically evaluated and solved through technology. In addition, husbands should be encouraged to assume an advocacy role on our behalf, becoming much more involved in their wives' health care. For too long, fathers have been treated as only observers of the process of childbearing.

More than ever, men and women are needed who will speak out on issues related to pregnancy, birth, and breastfeeding. That is why I remain actively involved as a childbirth educator and lactation consultant in my community. Consider the following paper I wrote several years ago in reaction to the doctor-sponsored classes: Are these

things any less true today than they were in 1980?
Are men and women such as myself any less
needed than we were *before* health care providers
started sponsoring their own classes? Printed for
the most part as it appeared as an editorial in the
International Childbirth Education Association's
Sharing,[3] I feel it's important to share it here
again with you:

My commitment to education for childbirth
primarily springs from my own experiences with
giving birth. What my beliefs boil down to at their
most basic level is this: that parturition involves a
woman's capacity to negotiate with her body as it
acts in a very powerful way. Her entire being is
exposed to the most fundamental and exquisite
sensations that she is ever likely to experience.
Yet, even a description such as this is mundane. If
giving birth makes a woman vulnerable, it makes
her valuable as well. Greeting one's child for the
first time face-to-face is awesome, incredible. To
be so much a part of another individual is
staggering. There is not one of life's "common"
experiences to compare with this, in my
estimation.

I am sorry for the women who create a great
distance between their bodies and their thoughts,
their children and themselves. As a childbirth
educator, I work to bridge those gaps, strive to
eliminate facades, and seek to nurture the innate
strength and courage that each woman often
buries under layers of cultural pretense. Preparing
women to give birth requires nothing less than
the most transparent kind of sharing, so that
expectant mothers can be convinced of how
important "opening up" can be. There is
no simple formula, no magical means of
communicating the terms of birth. Anyone who

attempts to slip women into neatly packaged and efficiently managed birth experiences commits a criminal act—for they are robbing women of discovering what only *they* should be allowed to negotiate: their passage into the role of mothering their children.

What we now have are many men who have defined the terms of birth from a variety of medical perspectives who lack the principle vantage-point of having the ability to give birth themselves. They are to be lauded for attempting to eliminate the hazards of birth and to minimize its risks, but these men often dictate the management of labor and control the passage of women through territory that is uniquely feminine. It is sheer folly. *How did we ever allow this to happen?*

Male supervision of birthing and nursing women is an invasion of privacy. Most women, if asked to be completely frank, will tell you there is something odd about males performing pelvic exams, vaginal checks, and perineal massage during labor, but it continues because we often have no alternative.

It is my perception that we will continue to experience this disparity between the medical management and the human experience of childbirth until women say that they require better treatment. The male bias in obstetrics, the economic system of health care in the U.S., and our cultural definition of childbirth as a risk-laden condition requiring medical intervention all prevent women from feeling whole as they give birth. Is it any wonder so many women are depressed afterwards?

Without knowing it, women are injured without being aware of the assault. Their babies are removed from their bodies, often surgically via episiotomies or by cesarean section, and returned only at "suitable" times. How this suitability is determined has little to do with how a mother feels and much to do with the efficiency of routinized institutional care. Why does it alarm us when mothers frequently feel *detached* rather than *attached* to their offspring?

I might not have encountered these issues if I had not personally experienced both obstetrically managed and home-oriented childbirth. I probably wouldn't realize the significance of human interaction without separation or interruption with two of my newborns until I compared it to giving birth to my second daughter only to have her taken out of sight and placed in a nursery. (I am not bitter, just wiser. I am also not a feminist in the usual sense of the word. I am simply thinking that justice is not rendered in the typical American birthing situation.)

These are things only a mother can know. It is a shameful thing that mothers have the least to say about them. As mothers, I hope you will care enough to represent these issues. As childbirth educators, I wish you continued insight into the significance of birth as a passage that mothers, fathers, and their children go through. May your vision remain unclouded by the "powers-that-be" so that you can touch the lives of others as they approach such a life-changing event.

Can you believe it? All this from a Christian mother who teaches a few classes each week, counsels women over the phone, and runs biweekly support groups for nursing mothers!

I once heard George Bernard Shaw quoted as having said that all professionals represent a conspiracy against the laity. To a certain extent, I fully concur. It has taken me more than a dozen years to be accepted as a "layperson" (someone who is neither a nurse nor a doctor) by the medical community, and to this day there are physicians in town who will not refer their clients to me. Even though I have the expertise in adult education, counseling skills, and breastfeeding assistance that their own office nurses lack, they are somehow threatened by not being able to control the information their clients receive.

How have I coped with all this foolishness? By studying diligently, taking certification exams, developing an individualized undergraduate major in Reproductive Health Education, teaching hundreds of classes, and forming real-life support groups for new mothers. Essentially, when you get right down to it, I've become something of a professional mother. Childbearing and mothering are the subjects I've studied for fifteen years, both as an observer and as a participant. If the medical community had any idea that all I was doing was recycling maternal wisdom gleaned from my accumulation of experiences and self-directed studies, I would be run out of town on the spot by those who deny that mothers can know anything vitally important about birthing, breastfeeding, and nurturing their babies.

Fortunately, there *are* nurses and physicians who have come to realize their limitations. They aren't averse to requesting my help when their clients need it and realize that the solutions I offer aren't based on anything weird or far-out, but are simply practical solutions given from a common-sense approach. In helping women to understand their ability to give birth and by supporting them in times of crisis as well as in times of success, women like myself make learning how to be a mother easier. We've found there's no better way to promote the health of mothers and babies than by enabling them to take care of themselves, with a little help from their friends.

> The woman who is herself emotionally healthy, senses by instinct and can soon learn by observation to know her own baby. . . . The essence of motherhood is creativeness, which is an instinctual gift. There are no set rules for the making of a great painting or the writing of a fine book or the composing of a great sonata. Yet a technique must be mastered. The depth of feeling which goes into creativeness cannot be measured out or indicated. This is determined by instinct. But whether mothering is done by instinct or design, it is important to know that it is as vital to the child's development as is food.[4]

This chapter is lovingly dedicated to Laura Rausher and women like her who promote the safety and dignity of home-centered maternity experience through their dedicated practice of midwifery.

ELEVEN

On Berkmeyer's Farm

Your silent love
Comes over me
In the stillness of my memory
I feel Your touch
I've heard Your call
Your silent love
Remains unchanged and strong.[1]

Russ Taff and friends

*L*AST NIGHT, I DROVE OUT TO A RURAL Nebraskan town (pop. 600), riding with a youth pastor from a large Lincoln church, a student teacher from the university, and the student's fianceé. We took off for our mission from a parking lot on the east side of town and proceeded to travel into the hills surrounding the city, away from traffic lights and other familiar signposts. Whenever I drive away from the city limits of this town, I immediately feel like I've fallen off the edge of the planet.

I grew up in metropolitan Detroit in a

neighborhood where the houses were about fifteen feet apart. I can't seem to remember anyone ever growing anything edible in the backyard. My high school graduating class had somewhere around 850 seniors in it, and consequently I felt most at home in large movie theaters, shopping malls, and public libraries. These memories of home are firmly rooted in the safely enclosed spaces and one-way streets of my childhood.

When our family moved to Nebraska in 1981, a friend wrote to tell me that when she thought of us she pictured the television show "Little House on the Prairie." It's not *that* prehistoric here. Especially not in Lincoln. But I must admit that there is a unique quality about life out in the small towns of this state that seems to foster both a pioneer spirit and community pride in many of its people. Even though I appreciate these traits and enjoy visiting new places, I sometimes feel like an alien peering out through a window in my spacecraft at a way of life that is completely foreign to me. I have discovered, however, that many of us speak the same language, which helps a lot.

The purpose of our journey was to present a Judeo-Christian view of human sexuality to a group of high school students at the farm home of a Mr. and Mrs. Berkmeyer. None of us had met any of the people we had been invited to share with. The superintendent of the school district had requested that we come out on a Wednesday to a gathering of the Fellowship of Christian Athletes to talk to about sixty to seventy-five students. Since there is a grand total of seventy-five students who attend Elmwood High School, this basically meant speaking to almost the whole student body. Imagine it: an entire high school's population all crowded into somebody's basement. Now you've got the picture about what I mean regarding how positively strange I often feel when I venture east of 84th Street.

Upon our arrival, we were greeted at the door of a beautiful brick house by a handsome, sandy-haired man who looked to be in his early forties. He had overalls on and appeared to have just completed a day of working out on his land. After quick introductions, he excused himself, explaining that he needed to go "wash up." When I saw him later that evening, I hardly recognized him with a clean, pressed shirt and dress pants on. He also appeared to have twice as much hair.

Mrs. Berkmeyer was attractively attired and busy in the kitchen, but paused to welcome us into her home and invite us to have a seat in the living room until the kids arrived. They gradually appeared through the front door, in groups of threes and fours. After stopping momentarily to say hello, they would then hurry into the basement. At the appointed time, my companions and I stepped downstairs to join them. I had a general idea of what I wanted to say to these young people, but when I saw them all packed together in a huge circle, shoulder to shoulder, a rather large lump found its way to the base of my throat.

This is going to be quite an evening. How did I manage to get myself into this? Who am I to inform these kids about their sexuality? What do they already know? Are their parents relieved by tonight's gathering? Am I fooling myself, or could this be an evening that many of them won't forget?

I noticed that the pastor of the only church in Elmwood, whom I had just met upstairs, was positioned alongside his wife on the far side of the room behind the Ping-Pong table. That didn't help my sense of composure any. I sat down and waited to be introduced, reviewing my notes and trying to figure out what to say. A few minutes later, it was my turn to be up front, both literally and figuratively, and open the evening's presentation. I grabbed my pile of books, swallowed hard, and attempted to reach my spot without stumbling.

I have made a variety of presentations on this topic, but never to a group this age. They're practically the same age as my daughters! Look at all these inquisitive faces . . . They are so young!

"I'm here tonight to talk to you about sexuality, and even more importantly, about how very much God loves you. Each of us here started out exactly the same way in terms of the facts of how our lives got started, yet look how different we are! There is *no one* just like you or me in the entire universe. What an amazing thought! That you and I began as two tiny cells, a sperm and an egg, and from that time on have continued to grow into the people we are today. Out of the millions and millions of sperm your father has produced and the hundreds of eggs your mother contains within her ovaries, only one cell from each of your parents joined together to become *you.*"

How can I adequately explain the magnificence of what I'm saying? Or dare to convey the beauty of conception with mere words? Each living being who is here tonight possesses something of you, God. The life we share finds its source in You! Life that cannot be bought, but is a gift . . . Your gift . . . Your stupendous, spectacular gift! Within a mother's egg cell, measuring just four-thousandths of an inch across, are packed twenty-three chromosomes containing half of all the information needed to produce a human being, a person who could one day be, like those of us here tonight, expressing what it means to be ALIVE. When joined to a male sex cell, with even smaller proportions, the most creative explosion in all of nature takes place.

"At the moment your life began, one of the most beautiful and fantastic scenes in all of creation took place within your mother. She wasn't even aware of this historic event! Deep inside her body, a troop of sperm from your dad traveled a long distance to reach an egg that had been released by one of your mom's ovaries. Only the strongest of your father's cells survived, and when they reached their destination, they eagerly clustered around their prize. *Only one* succeeded in breaking through the egg's protective barrier; then no more sperm were allowed inside. A biology teacher once told me he had once watched this process, called fertilization, using animal cells. He described it as one of the most powerful things he had ever seen. A burst of light, shooting colors out in all directions, heralded the conception he witnessed under the gaze of his microscope. Two separate cells merging into one new creation . . . The dawning of a brand-new life. That is how you and I began. Amazing, isn't it?"

Amazing? Try GLORIOUS! A fantastic voyage followed by a spectacle of such grandeur, so brilliantly composed that it's too incredible to fully comprehend it! "I will praise thee, O Lord, with all my heart . . . I will tell the story of thy marvelous acts."[2] Help me to say these things in such a way that it will be easier for us to remember Your abiding love for us!

"Now I want you to know that *all* teachers have a point of view when they teach about human sexuality. Mine is that I believe that the very first man and woman, named Adam and Eve, were created by the hand of God in His own image. These two books over here were written by people who refute this belief. They believe that human beings evolved from 'primal ooze' and, over millions of years, just happen to have turned out like you and me. I once heard someone compare this view of human life to being like a blown-up scrap heap ending up as a Cadillac. Yes, that *is* pretty absurd! What do you think happens to the way people view the value and meaning of human life if they believe we're only here *by accident?* Right! They conclude that what we say and do doesn't really matter. If we came from green slime and aren't heading anywhere after we die, then we're just like any other animal. Do you believe that? But did you know human beings are the *only* creatures capable of chastity? There's a good deal more we're capable of too. The Bible's view, that a personal Creator God made man and woman in His own image, changes the way we view *everything.* "

Where would I be tonight if it weren't for you, Lord? Would I be here on Berkmeyer's farm in Elmwood, Nebraska, out in the middle of nowhere, sharing my reason for hope and for living with these kids? Would I feel the aching in my heart that yearns to comfort and reassure each person here tonight? I want to reach out and touch every one of these children and take them in my arms, wrapping them up in the magnitude of Your love. Oh, God, adolescence is such a scary, painful, exciting time! But I know You will faithfully guard and watch over these kids as they continue to grow, and I am thankful.

"There is something else the Bible tells us about our lives. It doesn't only tell us where we came from and about God's love for us. It also tells us that the lives that began at the moment of conception in our mother's wombs are lives that *will never end.* Think of it! This rock I am holding is called a Petoskey stone, a rounded piece of fossilized coral said to be three hundred million years old. It's not really that old, but since current dating methods are based on a theory of evolution, that's how old a geologist at the University of Nebraska would say it is. So let's just suppose it's really *old.* Yeah . . . I mean, we are talkin' OLD here! Well, God's Word tells us that someday this rock will be considered YOUNG compared to you and me. That is what eternal life means . . . spending *eternity* with God! Don't worry if you can't completely understand 'forever' because only God has that totally figured out. What we *can* know for now is that what we say and do with our lives matters in respect to eternity. That includes what we say and do through our bodies, too."

Okay, this is what they came for. They've been waiting to hear what I'm going to say about their sexuality ever since they got here. Are they ever in for a surprise!

"When you were born, you came into the world with a God-created capacity for what we call *bonding.* As you left your mother's womb, you entered the world, opened your eyes 'outdoors' for the very first time, and took a great big breath. That breath changed your circulatory and respiratory systems by shutting a flap that, while open, had prevented you from breathing and consequently drowning in the amniotic fluid you had developed in within the uterus. With that one cry, you went from living in water to living in air! When your mom and dad spoke to you, your tiny head turned to listen because you recognized their voices even though you had never seen them before. Then they probably looked into your eyes to start to get to know you better, and you looked right back. That *really* impressed them, you know it? It impressed them so much that they began falling in love with you, like a special kind of 'love at first sight.' Even though they most likely started to bond with you *before* your birth, they had never seen you or touched you before. And when they touched you, they couldn't believe how soft and precious your skin was! Have you ever touched or smelled a newborn baby's skin? Then you already know what I'm talking about."

Now, don't start to cry. They already must think you're pretty crazy for agreeing to talk to the whole high school about sex. You've still got to tell them the most important thing of all. Take a deep breath . . .

"The ability to bond with someone else was placed in each one of us by our Creator as a very important part of who we are as people. Every baby that is born into the world comes with a capacity for loving that must be developed and nurtured over time, as well as having an *immediate* need to be loved right away from the first moment. The bonding that takes place between parents and their children at birth is an introduction to what it means to form an exclusive one-woman, one-man bond within marriage. Why do you think God wants us to wait until we get married to express our sexuality? Is it because God doesn't approve of sex? Let's look in the Bible and see . . .

'So God created man in his own image, in
the image of God he created him, male and
female he created them. . . .'

*Different yet similar . . . reflections of their
Maker . . .*

'God blessed them and said to them, "Be
fruitful and increase in number, fill the earth
and subdue it." '

*Children, blessings from God . . .
expressions of His life among us . . .*

'For this reason a man will leave his father
and mother and be united to his wife and
they will become one flesh. . . .'

*Marriage, divinely mysterious . . . leaving,
cleaving, joining . . .*

'The man and his wife were both naked and
they felt no shame. . . .'

*A gift to be celebrated! Received with joy!
Shared for a lifetime!*

"God created Eve to be the perfect partner for
Adam. It would have been neat to see his reaction
to the second person on earth. I bet he was pretty
excited! That's because God has given us the
ability to be attracted to members of the opposite
sex. What we need to remember is that the
special feelings God created us to have can create
a strong bond between two people. When we
become sexually intimate outside of marriage, we
weaken our ability to form an exclusive bond
within marriage. It's *impossible* to have sex with
someone and leave your soul parked outside the

door. What we do with our bodies affects our minds and our spirits in *all* cases.

"So avoid picturing God as a big mean ogre pointing down at you saying, 'No, no, no! Don't touch!' Try to imagine a tender Father instead, gently whispering: 'I love you, My precious child, and desire you to receive the good gifts I have created for you. One day it will be time for you to open up the gift of your sexuality and share it with the person you love enough to commit your life to. Because I have created you this way, please wait until then.'

"Some of you here tonight have already been sexually active. Some of you may have been sexually abused or assaulted. You don't need to continue living a life that causes you, or others, pain. Through Jesus, when we confess what we have done and what is on our hearts, we receive forgiveness, healing, and a fresh start. There will probably be many times when you will feel pressured, discouraged, tempted, confused. Always remember that you are not alone, that you have a Friend who will never forsake you. Draw close to Him, and He will draw close to you. He loves each one of you very, very much."

After I sat down, the youth pastor shared guidelines for sexual behavior from the Bible and directly challenged everyone there to live by God's "blueprints" for our lives. Then we split up into two groups. The boys went upstairs with the pastor, school superintendent, and student teacher. I remained in the basement with the girls, the pastor's wife, and Jimmy's fiancée. Much of what we discussed in our group revolved around mothering, surprisingly enough. All but one of the thirty or forty girls present said they hoped to be mothers someday. I couldn't help but think that the preceding discussion of human reproduction,

placed within a developmental sequence
beginning with the miracle of conception, had
struck a chord.

*It makes no sense at all to focus on just one
aspect of sex when, from the standpoint of
female sexuality, so much of our design was
created to be expressed in nurturing and being
sensitive to the bonding process. When we
abandon this as women, the "big picture" of
human sexuality is destroyed.*

I realized this once again last night and am
encouraged that many others who visited
Berkmeyer's farm felt that way, too.

> Build homes and plan to stay; plant
> vineyards. . . . Marry and have children, and
> then find mates for them and have many
> grandchildren. Multiply! Don't dwindle away!
> . . . For I know the plans I have for you, says
> the Lord. They are plans for good and not for
> evil, to give you a future and a hope.[3]

TWELVE

Reaffirming Traditional Mothering

The newborn baby brings with him to this life the pervasive quality that insures what is waiting for him (and waiting on him) in the needs and drives of individual women, in the tradition of generations of mothers, and in universal institutions of motherhood. [1]

Dr. Erik Erikson

"YOU CAN DO IT! IT'S NOT GOING TO BE MUCH LONGER . . . I know this is difficult for you, but your baby's almost here! That's your child's head you feel; just try to release *into* the pressure—don't resist it. There, that's great! Remember: each contraction is bringing you closer to your goal. Your baby will be here soon!"

All across the country, childbirth educators commonly call the most emotionally demanding phase of labor *transition*. It is the time during childbirth when the baby steadily presses the cervix open in the final part of the first stage of labor.

Ordinarily the uterus must make a concerted effort to accomplish its task as it stretches the cervix open to a full ten centimeters, a diameter of about four and a half inches. Characterized by strong, muscular contractions typically lasting from one to two minutes in length, this phase of labor is well known for its ability to produce a fierce backache, rectal pressure, fatigue, and feelings of self-doubt. A mother is likely to look at those who are accompanying her through labor and declare, "I can't do this anymore!" It's perfectly natural to want to give up, leave one's birthing bed, and forget about one's baby temporarily when the long contractions of transition occur with very little rest between them.

The word *transition* means to progress from one condition, state, or activity to another. The experience of childbearing involves a whole series of transitions following the act of love leading to a baby's conception. What begins as a dual effort, shared by a wife and her husband together, becomes an experience that physically affects the woman alone. The mutually enjoyed event that sparks the formation of a new life ushers in a nine-month waiting period involving major changes in a woman's mind and body as she prepares her heart and lifestyle for her baby's arrival. Pregnancy itself becomes a time of transition, especially with the first child, as a woman moves toward embracing her maternal role and new identity as a mother.

This time of anticipation and nurturing a preborn child culminates in the work of labor and birth as a woman progresses through the brief transition between pregnancy and actively mothering her baby at the breast. Although this reproductive phase in a woman's life lasts only for a matter of hours, it is a crucial turning point in her life.

All labors involve women in a time of sudden reservations and mixed feelings: at the very moment when a woman feels the least able to cope with her body, she must consciously decide to *let go* and fully allow herself to *give birth;* at a time when she feels the most detached from the child within her, she must decide to relate to her baby as a separate individual who is ready to leave her womb. The key to passing through this transition with dignity is to silently proclaim: "Yes, my child, I *am* ready for you! I am thankful for my God-given ability to birth you . . . How I want you to be born so that I can hold you in my arms at last!"

In the midst of this physical and emotional upheaval lies a deep spiritual truth. As a laboring woman surrenders herself to the powerful and sometimes frighteningly strong efforts of her body to give birth to her child, she finds joy awaiting her at the end of her toil. As she lays down her fears concerning the outcome of her labor and what the future may hold, she discovers a new type of courage she had never imagined herself capable of possessing. Little in life prepares us ahead of time for such a demanding, all-encompassing task! It is far from being a comfortable or serene process. But what a woman experiences during the transition phase of labor is the passage from a state of complete physiological intimacy with her child to a different kind of closeness as her baby emerges from her body.

Following this event comes a transition of another sort as a baby is eased into life outside the womb over a period of months and years. *The more a woman is willing to share her life with her first child during this time, the farther she will find herself from being the person she used to be.* Again, it is not a comfortable process. To fully bond to one's child requires the same kind of surrender and sacrifice as the transition phase of labor requires, even though it expresses itself differently.

Becoming a mother offers an unlimited opportunity for personal growth to a woman who is willing to *gradually* enable her child to move into a life of his or her own. The woman's identity is further transformed during this time. While allowing for a break with her past way of life, this "rite of passage" into the role of motherhood opens up new horizons for her future.

When we become mothers, past traditions, familiar role models, and the wide variety of maternal examples we have been exposed to throughout our lives merge with a new awareness of ourselves as we assume the central position in our *own* families as mothers. Over time, we learn how to incorporate our former ideas about what mothering involves with the day-to-day experience of motherhood. Entering this new territory involves risk-taking of the highest order! It is one of life's most significant passages, the transition between a relatively independent lifestyle to a period of mutual dependency with another person, unlike anything we have ever encountered before. When we assume the *full* responsibility for nurturing and caring for our babies and our children, we elect to take a giant step away from our own childhood and former way of life.

This does not happen automatically for any of us. There are no "natural" mothers. None of us are fully prepared for what to expect. The idea of the natural mother or instant mother or perfect mother is a *myth,* pure and simple. That is because *each* of us has to *learn* how to be a mother, just as we needed to learn how to be wives. Nowhere in the world do women just happen to become wonderful mothers overnight. But take heart: the healthy female body contains the original set of blueprints for conceiving, developing, bearing, and nurturing new life. Through responding to the wisdom of our Creator's design expressed within our bodies, it is possible to learn a great deal about how to lovingly respond to one's baby's needs, not only during pregnancy, but for a significant length of time afterwards as well.

Contrary to current public opinion, the roles of mothers and fathers were *not* created equal. When we use the term "to father," for example, a far different mental picture is painted in our minds than when we use the feminine equivalent "to mother." This is due to the fact that from a purely biological standpoint, *fathering* requires only that a man participate in the initial act of sexual intercourse, whereas *mothering* involves a distinctly separate set of interrelated reproductive responses on the part of a woman: ovulation, conception, implantation, gestation, parturition, and lactation.

The Judeo-Christian model of marriage and family life, based upon Biblical values that affirm these basic differences between mothering and fathering, fully supports the complementary nature of these activities. *The Word of God provides the moral framework within which family relationships can fruitfully thrive so that each member of a family benefits.* This truth is inescapable. No other view of the meaning and value of human sexuality even comes close to offering men, women, and children the protection, sanctification, and freedom that they need in order to live in harmony with one another or with the realities of their physical design. Marriages are blessed and nourished in a multitude of ways, even amidst the varied demands of family life, when a husband and wife commit themselves to fulfilling their God-created roles with the assurance that they are living in conformity with the Lord's pattern for their lives.

The expression of mothering through pregnancy, childbirth, and breastfeeding places many more physical demands on a woman than fathering does upon a man. In addition, the emotional, social, and spiritual impact of these reproductive states influence us far differently than they do our husbands.

We are living at a time and place in history that asks us to deny these fundamental differences, but tell me: does this make any sense to you at all? It seems that ever since the uniquely feminine functions of childbearing and breastfeeding were rendered optional through the abuse of contraception and infant formula, our society has placed less and less value on the worth of women who *choose* to marry, have children, and create nurturing home environments through homeworking rather than careerism. As a result, many women have found that taking a detour around our Creator's plan for their lives has brought heartache instead of fulfillment: a steep rise in the number of single-parent families, the inability to enjoy the infancy and childhood of one's offspring, and increased inner conflict regarding the meaning of womanhood.

Unlike women in many other places around the world, women in the United States can choose when and if they will have children, how many children to have, when to schedule a pregnancy so it is most convenient, whether to breastfeed or bottle-feed their infants, and who will take care of their babies if they choose to be away from the home for most of the baby's waking hours. We have an absolutely mind-boggling set of alternatives available to us!

If you doubt this, take a trip this afternoon to your local discount center or pharmacy and check out the number of bottle nipples currently on the market, displayed in a prominent position in the center of the baby department. You'll find nipples made of silicone as well as latex; orthodontic, natural, premature, juice, formula, and toddler nipples; with name brands including Playtex, Nuk, Playskool, Pur, and Evenflo on the labels. It's crazy! But even so, it's only the *human* nipple that doesn't need sterilizing and can't be pulled off.

Have all of these "choices" really enabled us to be better mothers? Of course not. As women, *most of us are already equipped with nearly everything our babies will need to promote their survival during the first six to nine months of life.* Since manufacturers can't make a profit off natural mothering, we will never see it promoted or advertised in the media. Think about it.

Unlike childbirth educators, when anthropologists refer to "transition" they use it to describe *the time between a baby's birth and the establishment of an infant's complete physiological separation from his or her mother.* Around the world, the average length of this phase is *two to three years* as a baby is gradually eased from total dependence upon the mother just before birth to weaning from the breast. In the case of many American women, this period of transition very often lasts all of *one minute,* until the umbilical cord is clamped and cut. Compare this to women belonging to the traditional culture of the Amayra in Bolivia:

Wherever the mother goes, even to dance, the baby will go with her, little head close to hers and slung forward in front of her in case of need. . . . No modesty is attached to nursing even in public places. . . . At night, the child sleeps next to his mother. This continues until he is about two years old or even until the next child is born. Nursing has precedence over any other activity in which the mother may be engaged, such as selling her vegetables in the market, for instance, although she may be extremely anxious to make the sale.[2]

In a Jordan village halfway around the globe, in a completely different ethnic group and culture, a similar pattern of traditional mothering has been reported:

Even after birth, the mother and child are closely connected for a long period. To be fed the baby requires its mother all the time, for it must not be hungry. Both in everyday life and at festivals, one can observe how, as soon as the child cries or shows the least sign of restlessness, it is at once laid on the mother's breast. Very often a woman who is nursing a child has an opening in her dress over each breast and thus she can feed it at once. And she does it unhesitatingly, in any place, at any time and very often.[3]

Still yet another example of this pattern of care was noted in China:

The mother puts her child to her breasts as often as he gets restless or cries, and this is day and night. Nobody can tell how often the infant is nursed or for how long. It is never limited to a few months, but lasts for years (five is no rarity). Usually the nursing period lasts until the birth of another child. It is looked at as very natural when the mother nurses her child and she therefore carries him always with her.[4]

In their elegant review of cross-cultural practices related to pregnancy, birth, and breastfeeding, psychologist Dr. Niles Newton and the late anthropologist Dr. Margaret Mead declared that the United States has a "severely muted transition period" in comparison to all of the other cultures in the world. In 1967, they found that this period lasted an average of *three weeks* in our culture.

We may well ask ourselves how this has affected the way women have come to view their maternal role and responsibilities in our culture since the turn of the century. According to Newton and Mead, "One of the most striking aspects of modern industrial culture is this muting of the transition phase. . . . The United States may be considerably ahead of other countries in the earliness of severance of the physiological relationship between mother and baby."[5] Furthermore, these two researchers, both mothers themselves, suggest that the cultural patterning of the transition period "may crucially influence subsequent [maternal-child] behavior," noting that in traditional cultures "close mother-baby contact, sensitivity to crying, child spacing, and prolonged breast feeding" are frequently grouped together as interrelated factors contributing to a much longer period of physical and emotional contact between mother and child.[6]

Newton and Mead go on to state, "More needs

to be known about what other factors in the total current cultural pattern correlate with a muted or a developed transition period. One key may be the way women's work is patterned, and also how much help they get from their family and wider social group during the time when they are physiologically connected with the fetus and the infant. We may also ask how the economic and work contributions expected of mothers with young infants are related to the type of care given and the muting or the developing of the transition phase."[7]

In regards to the way work is structured in America today, there is little if any difference between what is expected of female employees with infants and young children as compared to male workers. The average length of a woman's maternity leave is six weeks, and after this she is usually expected to assume the full responsibility for her work load once again. Since lactation is optional, babies do not accompany women to work in the vast majority of cases. Why should they? In an era of equal rights, the differences between the biological roles of males and females, and subsequently the value of breastfeeding and mothering, are totally ignored. Unless a woman chooses to work at home, she will find it necessary to find a substitute mother, or "caretaker," to fill in for her when she is absent. But what impact does this have on maternal-child relationships? Upon bonding? Upon families? Or on the ability of women to fundamentally change their identity in ways that allow them to closely become attached to their children through the hormonal and physical relationship with a baby that full-time breastfeeding produces?

Well-known pediatrician, researcher, and

author Dr. T. Berry Brazelton recently went on record as stating that six weeks *does not* provide a sufficient amount of time for a mother to satisfactorily develop a deep attachment to her baby. Along with several other imminent specialists in the field of early childhood development, he strongly believes that a one-on-one relationship between a mother and her infant is vitally important to a child's emotional well-being, as well as to maternal identity.

Brazelton himself is convinced that *a minimum of four months of full-time mothering* should be made available to women as a means of encouraging healthy maternal-child relationships. Consequently, he has become involved in promoting changes in labor laws to meet this need. Even so, many believe Brazelton's estimate is far too conservative.

The time has come for women to ask themselves: Can a mother who daily removes herself from the moment-to-moment needs of her infant ever fully assume an identity that allows her to become deeply attached to her child? Can children, who traditionally have been nurtured one-on-one by their mothers for a period of two to three years at the breast, suddenly be expected to thrive emotionally in their mother's absence? Are there not far-reaching and long-term consequences to both mothers *and* babies in a "severely muted transition period"? Might the abandonment of lactation through the use of artificial feeding ominously foreshadow the abandonment of gestation itself as artificial wombs become available?

According to Newton and Mead, there *is* a relationship between the biological state of lactation and the quality of mothering a baby receives, just as there is a relationship between the biological state of pregnancy and preparation for childbirth and motherhood:

> In contrast to the fully developed transition period and the varied patterns connected with it, the transition period may be patterned so that it virtually ceases to exist. Since modern technology has not yet invented a feasible substitute for gestation, pregnancy and childbirth cannot be easily muted, but substitutes for lactation have been invented, and the transition period of physiological dependence can be, and often is, eliminated.[8]

Let's take a closer look at this interrelationship for a moment. In reading the previous descriptions of nursing mothers in Bolivia, Jordan, and China, what was your reaction? For the majority of American and Western European women, their response is likely to be "NO THANKS!! Taking a baby *everywhere?* Nursing totally on demand, whenever a baby indicates an interest? For a period up to *five years?*"

Even though we may claim to believe that breastfeeding is the "natural way" to feed a baby, with the wide acceptance of artificial feedings it is no longer viewed as the *normal* way. If it was, none of us would think twice about a woman nursing her baby in a restaurant, at a beach, or in a library; if a woman nursed her baby six times within the same hour, we wouldn't even notice; and if a two-year-old climbed into mommy's lap for a drink of milk as well as a hug, we wouldn't be in the least bit uncomfortable.

On the other hand, let's consider the reality of how abnormal the act of breastfeeding has come to appear to those living in a culture with a severely muted transition period. Since breasts are now believed to primarily serve as erotic playthings for men, it is taboo for decent women to nurse their babies in public places; physicians routinely instruct mothers to nurse their babies no more often than once every two to three hours in the early months of an infant's life (and much less often once a baby reaches the ripe old age of four to six months); and the thought of a two-year-old receiving breast milk from his mother makes most people cringe.

The cultural patterning of breastfeeding—"the natural way"—has been lost since the turn of this century, except among women who have dared to ignore accepted practices and follow their hearts instead of public opinion. For their strange, "unnatural" behavior, these women are labeled "breastfeeding fanatics" when in fact they have *reaffirmed traditional patterns of mothering* that have existed since early Biblical times.

Just as bottles "liberated" women from the physiological and psychological demands that mothering placed upon them *after* birth, artificial or *in vivo* gestation will free them from the hazards and discomforts of nurturing an infant *before* birth. Sound far-fetched? Then pay heed to one woman's advocacy of a type of reproductive technology that could be implemented within ten to fifteen years:

> Artificial reproduction is not inherently dehumanizing. [That's what many have said about artificial feeding!] At very least, development of an option should make possible an honest re-examination of the ancient value of motherhood. . . . Until the decision not to have children or not to have

them "naturally" (i.e. through pregnancy vs.
by artificial or extra-utero gestation) is at
least as legitimate as traditional childbearing,
women are as good as forced into their
female roles.[9]

For those who claim that such an option
would spare women the "degradation and
humiliation of pregnancy and childbirth,"
artificial gestation will be the ultimate solution to
the "inequity" between males and females in
terms of their reproductive roles. While many
have believed that breast milk substitutes freed
women from being tied down to their babies,
reproductive technology will one day make
lovemaking, pregnancy, and childbirth *optional* as
well. We already have most of what will be
needed to *completely separate sex from
reproduction:* artificial insemination, test-tube
conception, surrogate motherhood (or "host
wombs"), genetic screening, and artificial feeding.
It is now possible to avoid heterosexual
intercourse and still become a mother or father,
for a man to donate semen before a sex change
operation and later be fertilized as a "woman"
with his own sperm, and for men to carry a
pregnancy in their abdominal cavity and be
delivered by cesarean section. The horrors of the
remaking of human reproduction are now upon us
after a decade of historic discoveries in the field
of reproductive technology in the 1970s.

If these things seem shocking to us today, or if
we find the idea of artificial gestation morally
repugnant, we can only imagine how abnormal a
severely muted transition period would have
appeared to our ancestors. In the same way that
we have come to view bottle feeding as "normal,"
one day artificial gestation may be viewed as

normal also, perhaps as soon as fifty years from now. In the next chapter I present such a scenario in the form of a future grandmother's journal. I only hope and pray that what I have imagined to be the logical conclusion to our current epidemic of sexually tramsitted diseases and the scientific quest for the transformation of human reproduction will never come to pass. It doesn't have to happen at all if enough people reject these options and demand that research in the field of artificial reproduction be stopped.

But before you are transported to the year 2022, let me once again emphasize that *the natural transitions between sexual intercourse, pregnancy, birth, breastfeeding, and early childhood form a cohesive physiological basis for the development of maternal-infant attachment as it gradually progresses from conception to weaning in the second or third year of life. No amount of technology will improve on this biologically determined pattern that was set in place by a personal Creator, nor can anything that is artificially produced fully replace the spiritual significance and the emotional satisfaction that these experiences can produce in a woman's life.*

With the abandonment of *any* of these dimensions of childbearing and nurturing comes the mutation or obliteration of a significant portion of a woman's sexuality. We cannot and should not argue with the sexual design of our bodies. There is wisdom to be found in living out the fullness of our identity as wives and mothers through embracing the totality of our womanhood as it was created to be expressed. Even though traditional patterns of childbearing will be challenged by reproductive technology in the twenty-first century, just as traditional patterns of mothering were challenged in the twentieth, there is still time to halt the steady progression of genetic and reproductive alternatives if we make our opinions known. I urge you to thoughtfully consider what will happen if we don't.

> The breast was "intended" [i.e., created] to bind the baby and his mother for the first year or two years of life. If we read the biological program correctly, the period of breastfeeding insured continuity of mothering as part of the formation of human bonds. A baby today experiences many more separations from his mother than the baby in traditional breastfeeding societies. How does this affect the stability of bonds to mother? . . . The baby's rudimentary love language belongs to an innate repertoire. It is all there, potentially, in the program, but it must be elicited by a partner.[10]
>
> Dr. Selma Fraiberg

THIRTEEN

A Grandmother Remembers

*T*he spectacle of two young women giving
the breast to their babies made her blush
and turn away her face. She had never seen
anything so indecent in her life. And what
made it worse was that, instead of tactfully
ignoring it, Bernard proceeded to make open
comments on this revoltingly viviparous
scene. . . .

"What a wonderfully intimate relationship,"
he said, deliberately outrageous. "And what an
intensity of feeling it must generate! I often
think one may have missed something in not
having had a mother. And perhaps you've
missed something in not being a mother,
Lenina. Imagine yourself sitting there with a
little baby of your own. . . ."

"Bernard! How can you? . . . Let's go away,"
she begged, "I don't like it."[1]

Aldous Huxley,
Brave New World

*J*OURNEY WITH ME NOW *to the year 2022 for a look
at what might become of motherhood in our
lifetime. Brace yourself as you reflect on the*

carefully recorded thoughts of a sixty-nine-year-old grandmother on the eve of her first great-grandchild's arrival, as she considers the transformation that has taken place in human reproduction since her daughter was born in 1972.

So much has changed since I first held Joanna in our cherrywood bed at Predmore Farm fifty years ago. . . .

How archaic everyone thinks I am for choosing to bring my daughter into the world so "haphazardly" in light of what my great-granddaughter's arrival is going to be like! In spite of what I think and feel about today's birthing methods, my family is expecting me to be excited about tomorrow's decanting celebration. I'm sorry, but I just can't see it from their point of view at all.

For one thing, I can easily remember a time when women considered it a *blessing* to carry new life within their wombs. Being pregnant was one of life's most significant experiences. None of us back then realized how rapidly that view would disintegrate in the wake of the burgeoning field of reproductive technology, nor did we have any idea what the fallout would be from the dramatic rise in infertility cases resulting from the millions of women who contracted chlamydia and gonorrhea in the late 1900s. As greater and greater numbers of women were rendered sterile by these diseases and by using abortifacients as contraceptives (IUD's, morning-after pills, etc.), we could never have imagined how these social trends would eventually affect the way our grandchildren would come to view childbearing.

How could we have known that the popularization of *elective* sterilization would pave

the way for the *mandatory* sterilization of
adolescent boys and girls at the age of sixteen
today? When I was a young woman, millions of
men and women obtained vasectomies and tubal
ligations as the ideal solution to the "problem" of
fertility. Now *no one* considers it to be useful or
healthy to be fertile as an adult. After our youth
have deposited a prescribed number of sperm or
ova into tax-deductible storage for later use, why
would they? Before the turn of the century, the
ability to reproduce was viewed as a mixed
blessing and a moral quagmire by all but the most
conservative within our society. For over two
decades now the younger generation continues to
congratulate itself for having arrived at the perfect
way of avoiding this dilemma.

Expectant parents now steadfastly refuse to
leave conception and fetal development to
"chance." They feel it is their civil *right* to be
spared the personal tragedy associated with
unplanned pregnancies, birth defects, and
developmental disabilities. In addition, they are
more than happy to be able to select the gender
of their future offspring, as well as a wide variety
of their children's genetic traits. Even the March
of Dimes, an association I once worked with to
promote breastfeeding, went out of business ten
years ago due to the virtual elimination of all
miscarriages, birth defects, and numerous
genetically-linked syndromes and diseases.

Looking back, it seems strange that most of us
were unable to read the writing on the wall when
artificial insemination, now called *AI,* became
increasingly popular in the seventies and eighties.
At the time, who would have guessed that making
love would become as divorced from the moment
of conception as it is today? Once people began
to more clearly recognize the moral and legal

issues involved with *AI,* surrogate motherhood,
lesbian pregnancy, and host wombs were *already*
being widely covered in newspapers, magazines,
and on television. The demand for these
reproductive alternatives was too high for science
to ignore. These proved to be short-lived trends,
however. They were quickly superseded by a far
more lethal array of options that later sounded the
death-knell for the natural biological processes
involved in human reproduction.

Among the steps taken that moved our society
toward a philosophy of "reproductive autonomy"
in the years following the popularization of *AI*
was *in vitro* fertilization, which became widely
known when the first "test-tube" baby, Louise
Brown, was born in July 1978. By 1980, nearly
two hundred successful embryo transplants had
taken place around the globe—in Australia,
Canada, England, and France, as well as in the
United States. One wonders why prolife advocates
concentrated so heavily on the issue of abortion
when a holocaust that would eventually become
much more devastating was so obviously
developing . . . Abortion turned out to be merely
the tip of the iceberg.

Five years after Louise arrived, physicians in
Los Angeles achieved another significant
breakthrough when they used semen to perform
AI in the host womb of a surrogate mother and
then subsequently flushed the fertilized ovum
from her uterus before it could implant itself.
They then made medical history (but not the
evening papers) when they transplanted the tiny
zygote into the womb of the sperm donor's sterile
wife. Yet another landmark case had taken place
in the field of reproductive technology that the
public knew little or nothing about. Physicians
considered this type of embryo transplant, which

resulted from *in vivo* fertilization (in a human body instead of a test tube), to be much safer because it was entirely nonsurgical. Also, the ethical and legal problems which had begun to be associated with long-term host wombs were avoided.

For quite a while, the general public remained in the dark concerning these procedures until the famous custody battle over "Baby M" was brought to trial. It became widely known that women who either could not or would not bear a child were paying large sums of money to other women in what were essentially "Rent-A-Womb" business deals.

This seemed to work for a large number of couples until a woman named Mary Beth Whitehead came along. Mary Beth, who was mistakenly called a "surrogate mother," was actually the *real* mother of a child that resulted from Mary Beth's ovum being artificially inseminated with the sperm of William Stern. However, since Mr. Stern and his wife Ellen had acquired Mary Beth's signature on a contract stating that she would give the baby to the Sterns after giving birth, the Sterns claimed that the baby belonged to them even though Mary Beth later had second thoughts, refused her fee, and wanted to keep her baby.

Renting women's wombs turned out to be messy business, needless to say, and infertility specialists continued to search for ways to avoid such situations. Most people consider today's options to be a vast improvement over methods used in the twentieth century at the dawn of reproductive technology.

Our current policy of "harvesting" ova from the ovaries of sixteen-year-old women after inducing "multiple ovulation" with an injection of hormones avoids many complications. This, physicians claim, ensures that the ova will be collected at the peak of their existence and minimizes their exposure to chemical and environmental agents that could otherwise produce significant cellular damage to the ova later in a woman's life.

Likewise, young men of the same age normally place semen in local storage banks designed for this purpose. These are found in most communities under the name Conception Designs, Inc. or Cryogenic Resources Unlimited. With the AIDS crisis that developed in the late 1900s, no one blinked an eye when CDI opened the first center in its now nationwide chain eighteen years ago. By then, "body fluids" testing had become a well-known requirement of health insurance policies, and semen had become a household word.

Due to the tremendous advances in genetic research that were pioneered during the latter part of the twentieth century, all ova and sperm (now referred to as *gametes*) must today be screened for possible genetic abnormalities prior to being placed in long-term storage. Couples who wish to have children are required to obtain clearance before their gametes can be used for fertilization. All health insurance companies automatically cancel their coverage on anyone who fails to fulfill this requirement. Consequently, few men and women elect to accept the financial burden of paying for their own health care or the medical care that might be needed if they had a handicapped child. Genetic screening is a way, health insurance companies claim, of enabling all children to have the right to be protected from such conditions as spina bifida,

Down's syndrome, sickle-cell anemia, and cystic fibrosis.

Research that might have led to the discovery of the means to enhance the health of individuals with these conditions was abandoned once it was no longer viewed as being either morally or economically justifiable. As a result, we've arrived at a rather extreme "cure." But most citizens hail this as being a tremendous advance in the area of public health and as preferable to the use of such horrible practices as amniocentesis, D & E abortions, and "salting out" a handicapped fetus with saline. Even though a significant number of us repeatedly pointed out the barbarity of such practices in the old days, so-called "enlightened" medical professionals later manipulated our arguments by claiming that they *agreed* with us and were subsequently developing much more "humane alternatives." Were *we* ever naive!

Genetic screening became federally mandated a decade after the Reproductive Safety Act was passed in 1992. Originally designed as a way of minimizing the transmission of AIDS by requiring quarterly blood testing for all residents and visitors entering the U.S., the RSA was aimed at also reducing discrimination against individuals who were "at-risk" for developing AIDS. AIDS testing became mandatory for *everybody*. Once 250,000 people had contracted AIDS and the Department of Health and Human Services was besieged with escalating costs for treating AIDS victims, the public seemed to be more than willing to accept this policy, even though they didn't entirely approve of the National Reproductive Health Registry's efforts.

Eventually the agency changed its name to the National Registry for Reproductive and Genetic

Health without much fanfare. At the same time, it became a division of the National Institutes of Health, after a stint with the Centers for Disease Control in Atlanta.

Through a massive educational campaign aimed at promoting "healthy lifestyles," the NRRGH convinced youth that they have the right to understand their "genetic potential" and the unfavorable traits and diseases that they might be capable of transmitting to their children.

Our nation's young people seem relieved. Now *anyone* can become a parent, whether they have a poor health or genetic history or not, since gametes from anonymous donors are available for them to use, even if they aren't able to use their own. Whether single or married, fertile or infertile, straight or gay, parenting is an available option for everybody. Personally, I will never forget how most of my generation felt about the possibility of conception without having sex, but sex today is no longer defined in such "biologically limited" terms.

And so tomorrow afternoon my daughter's first grandchild will make her exit from what my granddaughter jokingly refers to as her "womb with a view," where her baby has been developing for the past nine months. Unlike the rest of us, our newest family member was conceived by *AI* in a private geneticist's office downtown, using gametes placed in storage eight years ago by my granddaughter and the baby's father. After spending several weeks in a laboratory to determine its normalcy, the zygote was then transferred to an *APS* in my granddaughter's home. This thoroughly modern device was initially developed as a way to enhance the development of premature babies and was put together in its early form at the National Institute of Heart and Lung Disease in Maryland way back in the 1970s. Originally called an Artificial Placentation System, it is now known simply by its initials as *APS*.

In 1973, few of us were aware that a documentary film was released and shown in university embryology classes that revealed an *APS* being used to grow lamb fetuses in. The film was quickly withdrawn from circulation, however, because scientists feared the possibility of a public outcry against the eventual application of an *APS* to humans.

The research continued behind closed doors for another thirty years, and by 1998 yet another historic event in the field of reproductive technology had taken place when the first baby was "born" after developing in an *APS* device. How long ago that seems! In just twenty-four years, "the *APS* alternative" has become so widely accepted that it is now viewed as the "normal" way to bring a baby into the world and is the method *most* women select as a result.

This high-tech, low-risk version of a woman's uterus, women claim, offers their babies all the advantages of an intrauterine pregnancy while eliminating most of its hazards. My granddaughter loves to remind me that unlike women in my day, *she* doesn't have to worry about an unplanned pregnancy, unsightly weight gain, or unnatural procedures being performed on her body. When episiotomies became "normal" and the cesarean rate rose to nearly 25 percent while I was a young woman, I protested too, but in a far different way than women of my granddaughter's generation have! She finds it incredible that women of my era put up with such assaults on their bodies for the sake of bringing new life into the world or that they were willing to carry babies that they knew neither the sex nor the condition of. "After all, Gran," she says, "my work schedule is unaffected by a pregnant mind-body state, and Garrett is able to bond with the baby as closely as I am. And no childbirth pain! Isn't it great?"

No, it isn't. I hate the way that thing looks, with its simulated maternal heartbeat thumping away as if my granddaughter's heart is incapable of doing a better job. It's kind of like a specialized type of aquarium, sitting over in the corner of her living room, waiting until its appointed time of departure.

I've tried to describe how I felt about being pregnant and the joy I experienced when I gave birth to my children to my granddaughter, but she can't relate to what I'm saying at all. She only smiles, half-listening to what I have to say, and then tells me my views are too "traditional" for her tastes. I often end up keeping my thoughts to myself and quiet my heart with the still vivid memories of nursing in my rocking chair while singing songs to my little ones as they drifted off to sleep at my breast.

After centuries of dreams and wishful thinking, science has finally brought us to the logical conclusion of its attempts to reshape and perfect man. I fear it will go even farther now that cloning has been patented. But I remember when things used to be different: when I held my children in my arms after bringing them into the world according to God's design for my life, and caring for them each day until they were grown, and weeping when they left the warmth of our home. And I wonder: what will become of my great-granddaughter's children once motherhood becomes obsolete?

Mothers and fathers, brothers and sisters. But there were also husbands, wives, lovers. There were also monogamy and romance.

"Though you probably don't know what those are," said Mustapha Mond.

They shook their heads.[2]

Aldous Huxley, *Brave New World*

FOURTEEN

Vision
for the
Future

*There is a difference between an ideal and a
vision. An ideal has no moral inspiration;
a vision has.*[1]

Oswald Chambers

THE THEMES PRESENTED IN THIS BOOK have ranged
from the commonplace to the extraordinary,
from everyday events to once-in-a-lifetime
experiences, from the peace and quiet of a
mother's arms to the fury and frustration of a
mother's broken heart. These chapters were
intended to be thought-provoking and motivating
to women who will read these very personal
views of what mothering has meant to me.

It is my belief that each baby arrives in this
world with a capacity to teach others about love
and with the ability to draw that love out of the
hearts of their mothers. Babies were created to
arrive with a thirst for maternal love, needing to
discover what it means to trust another, to be
cared for, to be nurtured, and protected. Why did

God make babies with such needs? Whom has He chosen with the primary ability to meet them? And most importantly, how are mothers responding to these questions—with their hearts or according to what is currently in fashion?

Regardless of what society comes up with in terms of "reproductive alternatives," day-care provisions, and family-oriented legislation, most mothers are the ones who can best nurture their *own* children emotionally, physically, and spiritually. Although many women choose to either mute or obliterate their innate capacity for mothering, many of us have chosen to respond to this dimension of our womanhood with fullness of heart and sincerity of purpose. While many men totally deny or ignore their wives' unique potential for creating a strong family through the expression of bearing and nurturing new life, millions of others faithfully guard the beauty of motherhood by loving their wives and working diligently to provide for their families.

The future need not end up with the disappearance of what so many of us believe is good and healthy and *right* about our lives. Often when things seem to be the most upside-down and confusing, the time is ripe for change and for taking action. *That time is now.*

It is time to acknowledge and share with others that *pregnancy is an event to be celebrated with joy and that giving birth is a landmark event in the history of a family.* It is time to recognize and take issue with the fact that *our culture sorely fails to meet the needs of mothers who choose to stay with their children rather than sending them to "daytime orphanages" for most of their waking hours.* It is time to admit that *for over the past fifty years the professional medicalization of childbearing and breastfeeding deprived an entire generation of women from experiencing these dimensions of their sexuality in meaningful and rewarding ways.* It is time to *confirm the uniqueness of breast milk as the ideal food for human infants and to affirm the emotional bond produced through breastfeeding in a way that no other method can duplicate.* It is time for us to *actively provide support, encouragement, and expertise to one another based upon our own rich and varied maternal experiences and to stop denying the incredible value of our mothering "know-how."* And finally, it is time for *you* to *join those of us who are addressing these concerns on behalf of the children among us.*

The little ones of our nation are not being served well by our society's inability to extend a warm welcome to its most vulnerable members, and it is even less likely to do so in the future unless we begin to act on our beliefs *now.*

Rather than thinking that future reproductive technologists will succeed in destroying the intrinsic worth and beauty of motherhood, let us begin to work toward creating a better world in which mothers can truly thrive, a world in which women are *rewarded* and *respected* for bringing new life into the world and for nurturing their children on a full-time basis. In this world, I envision women being encouraged to respond to their God-given capacity for fruitfulness with joy and dignity. Instead of economic opportunities being limited to a marketplace mentality, in my dream I picture women creatively developing ways to generate income through home-based or part-time businesses, services, and manufacturing companies. In this hoped-for future, I see *thousands* of women choosing to return to their homes and neighborhoods to build lasting relationships within their families and local communities as they participate in the daily lives of those around them.

This dream of mine is not a return to the suburban materialism of "The Donna Reed Show" that would have women return to measuring their success by how spotless their floors are or what brand of clothing their kids wear. Instead, it is a picture of *a way of life that places a higher value on people than on the value of owning things.*

What might be the result of such a mentality? Thriving community centers . . . care of the homeless, elderly, and shut-ins . . . talents expressed through counseling, writing, teaching, healing, guiding, nurturing, and producing worthwhile goods and services . . . home-based study, learning, and research . . . arts and crafts festivals sharing the work of "common" artists and craftspeople . . . *the home once again established as the creative center of life.* Isn't this what *really* matters when it comes to loving our children and loving our neighbors?

I recently sat in the middle of a small support group of women and their babies, aged five weeks to nine months, as they shared their joys and frustrations about mothering and breastfeeding. Although our group ran to just past 9 o'clock, a time when most infants tend to get tired and fussy, I heard no crying, distress, or upset expressed. Contentedly placed at their mommy's breast at the earliest signal of hunger or loneliness, each was perfectly happy to be held in Mother's arms near the calm steadiness of her heartbeat or to crawl near her feet on the floor. The room was filled with the sweet sounds of my young friends as they smiled and cooed and gurgled. *Being in the presence of new life is a privilege.* What can compare with the value of such a gift? Or who could possibly improve upon the grand design of maternal experience by reshaping what has already existed for centuries?

If we fail to recognize that mothering is an art which has a profound impact upon our entire society, or that the quality of our home lives deeply affects our communities, we are in danger of losing something very precious indeed. Let us open our eyes and once again embrace the true nature of traditional mothering as it is revealed in the developmental pattern formed by lovemaking, conception, birth, and breastfeeding, a sequence determined not by human design but by the loving hand of God.

While the world will go on without us for now, our sons and daughters will only be with us for a brief time. As they move into our lives and out of our homes, may we learn to joyfully celebrate and more fully recognize the opportunity we have been given to be able to set them on a course that will guide them for the rest of their lives. Thank God for the incredible vocation of motherhood!

The family is the place where loyalty, dependability, trustworthiness, compassion, sensitivity to others, thoughtfulness, and unselfishness are supposed to have their roots. *Someone* must take the initiative and use imagination to intentionally teach these things. . . . Love isn't just happiness in ideal situations with eveything going according to daydreams of family life or married life or parent-child closeness and confidences. Love has *work* to do! Hard and sacrificial work— going on when it would be easy to be provoked and think evil. Love takes imagination and the balance of putting first

things first to be taught to young people in
their formative years. . . . Can human love be
perfect? No, but it is meant to portray
something within the family of the love
of God for His Family. What is a family?
*A formation center for human
relationships—worth fighting for, worth
calling a career, worth the dignity of hard
work.* [2]

Edith Schaeffer

Notes

INTRODUCTION
1. Selma Fraiberg, *Every Child's Birthright: In Defense of Mothering* (New York: Basic Books, 1977).
2. Sheila Kitzinger, *Women As Mothers* (New York: Vintage, 1980), pp. 231, 232.
3. Joni Mitchell, "Big Yellow Taxi." Siquomb Publishing, 1969.

CHAPTER 1: TO AN EXPECTANT MOTHER
1. Mari Hanes, *The Child Within* (Wheaton, IL: Tyndale House, 1979), p. 1.
2. *Ibid.,* p. 34.

CHAPTER 2: THE BIRTHING BED
1. Nell Dorr, *Mother and Child,* 2nd edition (San Francisco: Scrimshaw Press, 1972).

CHAPTER 3: SNUGGLES
1. Elise Arndt, *A Mother's Touch* (Wheaton, IL: Victor Books, 1984), p. 17.

CHAPTER 4: AFFECTING ETERNITY
1. John Jefferson Davis, *The Christian's Guide to Pregnancy and Childbirth* (Westchester, IL: Crossway Books, 1986), pp. 40, 147.
2. Psalm 94:18, 19, NEB.
3. Psalm 116:5-7, NEB.
4. Psalm 138:8, NEB.
5. Psalm 143:6, 8, NEB.

CHAPTER 5: OF LULLABIES AND EXULTATIONS
1. Written by Ann Omley, 1944.
2. Written by Laurie Klein. Date unknown.

CHAPTER 6: HEART THOUGHTS
1. C. S. Lewis, *Mere Christianity* (New York: Macmillan, 1976), p. 182.
2. Psalm 86:15, NASB.
3. *Op. cit.,* Lewis, *Mere Christianity,* p. 188.

CHAPTER 7: OUT OF THE CABBAGE PATCH AND INTO THE GARBAGE PAIL
1. From Malcolm Muggeridge, *Something Beautiful for God* (New York: Harper and Row, 1971), p. 100.
2. *Mother Teresa* "Love Begins at Home," *Equipping the Saints Magazine,* Vol. 1, No. 3 (May/June 1987), p. 7.

CHAPTER 8: UNSUNG HEROES
1. George Gilder, *Sexual Suicide* (New York: Quadrangle, 1973), pp. 87, 88.
2. Eugene H. Peterson, *A Long Obedience in the Same Direction* (Downers Grove, IL: InterVarsity Press, 1980), p. 130.

CHAPTER 9: STRANDED BUT NEVER ALONE
1. Dr. Donna Ewy, *Preparation for Parenthood* (New York: Plume, 1985), p. 156.
2. Polls cited in K. Haas and A. Haas, *Understanding Sexuality* (St. Louis: Times Mirror/Mosby, 1987), p. 157.
3. Romans 12:2, *Phillips.*

CHAPTER 10: A CIRCLE OF CARING
1. Dr. Dana Raphael, *The Tender Gift* (New York: Schocken, 1973), p. 167.
2. *Psychology Today,* April 1987, p. 18.
3. ICEA *Sharing,* 8, January 1981.
4. Dr. Margaret Ribble, M.D., *The Rights of Infants,* 2nd ed. (New York: Signet, 1965), pp. 15, 16.

CHAPTER 11: ON BERKMEYER'S FARM
1. From "Silent Love," by P. and E. Janz, Russ and T. Taff, and C. Grossman Puig. Bug 'n Bear Music, 1985.
2. Psalm 9:1, NEB.
3. Jeremiah 29:5, 6, TLB.

CHAPTER 12: REAFFIRMING TRADITIONAL MOTHERING
1. Dr. Erik Erikson, quoted in T. Berry Brazelton, *On Becoming a Family* (New York: Delacorte, 1981), p. 105.
2. Margaret Mead and Niles Newton, "Cultural Patterning of Perinatal Behavior," in *Childbearing: Its Social and Psychosocial Aspects,* S. Richardson and A. Guttmacher, eds. (New York: William and Wilkins, 1967), pp. 177, 178.
3. *Ibid.,* p. 178.
4. *Ibid.*
5. *Ibid.,* pp. 181, 182.
6. *Ibid.*
7. *Ibid.,* pp. 186, 187.
8. *Ibid.,* p. 181.
9. Shulamith Firestone, *The Dialectic of Sex* (New York: Bantam, 1971), pp. 198, 199.
10. Dr. Selma Fraiberg, *Every Child's Birthright: In Defense of Mothering* (New York: Basic Books, 1977), pp. 28, 29.

CHAPTER 13: A GRANDMOTHER REMEMBERS
1. Aldous Huxley, *Brave New World* (New York: Harper and Row, 1946), pp. 130, 131.
2. *Ibid.,* p. 45.

CHAPTER 14: VISION FOR THE FUTURE
1. Oswald Chambers, *My Utmost for His Highest* (New York: Dodd, Mead and Co., 1930), p. 130.
2. Edith Schaeffer, *What Is a Family?* (Old Tappan, NJ: Revell, 1975), pp. 83, 90-92. Italics mine.